HOLT

American Anthem

HOLT, RINEHART AND WINSTON

A Harcourt Education Company

Orlando • **Austin** • New York • San Diego • London

Contents

The World Before 1600

Test Preparation

DIRECTIONS Read each question and circle the letter of the best response.

1. Which of the following could be a piece of archeological evidence?
   A a clay pot
   B an opinion
   C a harvest festival
   D a story of conquest

2. Why was the slash-and-burn technique effective?
   A Fires drove wild animals into large nets.
   B The ashes made the soil fertile.
   C It was useful for catching fish.
   D Fire was necessary for hunting and gathering.

3. Why was the sea level lower during the Ice Age?
   A Much of the earth's water was consumed by woolly mammoths.
   B Most of the earth's water had evaporated into the atmosphere.
   C Most of the earth's water was in underground lakes.
   D Much of the earth's water was frozen.

4. The Maya did which of the following?
   A built dwellings made of adobe
   B developed a writing system and a number system
   C used irrigation systems to farm the desert
   D founded Tenochtitlán, today's Mexico City

5. Which of the following groups lived in South America?
   A Olmec
   B Aztec
   C Inca
   D Maya

6. The Hopi, Apache, and Navajo peoples lived in what region?
   A the Southwest
   B the Northwest
   C the Eastern Woodlands
   D the Great Plains

7. What was special about the Iroquois people of the Northeast?
   A They built large adobe houses.
   B They were nomads who followed huge herds of buffalo.
   C They were an alliance of several different groups.
   D They came from Mexico.

8. Native peoples in North America shared what characteristic?
   A a style of building houses
   B a desire to grow crops
   C a clan structure based on the father's family
   D a connection to the natural world

9. What goods were the basis of most of the trade in West Africa?
   A salt and spices
   B gold and salt
   C buffalo and gold
   D beads and weapons

10. Islam was carried to West Africa by what group of people?
    A Spanish traders
    B Portuguese traders
    C Arab traders
    D British traders

11. Who performed the labor on the new Portuguese and Spanish plantations?
    A enslaved Africans
    B salt traders
    C European explorers
    D African royalty

The World Before 1600

12. Use the chart below to answer the following question.

CAUSES AND EFFECTS OF THE ATLANTIC SLAVE TRADE

CAUSES
- Settlers in the Americas needed many workers for labor-intensive plantation agriculture.
- Planters wanted cheap labor.

EFFECTS
- Historians estimate that 20 million Africans landed in the Americas.
- Historians estimate that millions of Africans died on slave ships crossing the Atlantic.

What is another possible effect that could be listed in the Effects box?
A Slavery became unpopular and disappeared in the Americas.
B Enslaved Africans started their own businesses and succeeded.
C The American economy became dependent on slavery.
D New crops made slavery useless.

13. What characterized the period called the Renaissance?
A learning and creativity
B calls for reform of the Roman Catholic Church
C an emphasis on logic and reason
D the domination of African kingdoms by European nations

14. What was the importance of the caravel?
A It allowed a single farmer to plow an entire field.
B It allowed explorers to travel around the globe much faster.
C It allowed horses to pull more weight.
D It allowed people to measure time.

15. Who led northern Europe after the Reformation?
A Catholics
B Africans
C Protestants
D explorers

16. Who built a settlement in Greenland in the year 985?
A the Spanish
B the Portuguese
C the Vikings
D the English

17. When Christopher Columbus sailed west, he expected to encounter what body of land?
A Africa
B Asia
C the West Indies
D North America

18. What best describes the practice of colonization?
A sailing across the Atlantic to find Asia
B establishing a system of agriculture
C exchanging foods and technologies
D establishing permanent colonies

19. What items did Native Americans receive as part of the Columbian Exchange that might have affected their lives?
A tomatoes, corn, and peanuts
B domesticated animals and guns
C squash, guns, and gold
D caravels and maps

20. **Expository Writing** Write a brief essay describing how the development of plantations led to the massive movement of Africans during the 1500s and 1600s.

European Colonies in America

Test Preparation

DIRECTIONS Read each question and circle the letter of the best response.

1. In 1521, the Aztec capital was conquered by explorers from which country?
   A Portugal
   B France
   C Spain
   D England

2. Besides finding gold, the conquistadors were also interested in which of the following?
   A circumnavigating the globe
   B spreading Christianity
   C finding religious freedom
   D discovering a northern route to Asia

3. Who was the first Spanish explorer to reach mainland North America?
   A Hernán Cortés
   B Juan Ponce de León
   C Francisco Vásquez de Coronado
   D Sir Francis Drake

4. In 1680 the Pueblo Indians revolted against which of the following?
   A the Spanish missionary system
   B King Philip's War
   C the use of indentured servants
   D the Treaty of Tordesillas

5. Why was the location of the Jamestown colony a problem?
   A The cold weather froze most of the crops.
   B It was inside the territory of several Native American tribes that were at war with one another.
   C The settlers were unable to grow crops in the rocky New England soil.
   D It was a low, swampy area filled with malaria-carrying mosquitoes.

6. Read the following quote about the causes of Bacon's Rebellion and answer the question that follows.

> First, The extreme low price of tobacco, and the ill usage of the planters in the exchange of goods for it, which the country, with all their earnest endeavors, could not remedy. Secondly, The splitting the colony into proprieties, contrary to the original charters; and the extravagant taxes they were [charged]. Thirdly, The heavy restraints and burdens laid upon their trade by act of Parliament in England.

   Which of the following sentences could also be part of this quote?
   A "Fourthly, The good nature of the frontier settlers."
   B "Fourthly, The disturbance given by the Indians."
   C "Fourthly, The poor soil and low rainfall in Virginia."
   D "Fourthly, The peaceful relations between settlers and Indians."

7. Which event opened the Atlantic Ocean and North America to English colonizing expeditions?
   A the conquest of the Aztec
   B the signing of the Treaty of Tordesillas
   C the discovery of gold in Mexico
   D the defeat of the Spanish Armada

8. How was the colony of New York unusual?
   A in the diversity of its settlers
   B in its political structure
   C in its prohibition of slavery
   D in the extent of its religious toleration

9. What was the House of Burgesses?
   A a center for selling tobacco
   B the governor's home in Virginia
   C the English court system
   D America's first legislature

10. How did the Pequot War end?
   A with the intervention of the French
   B with a brutal massacre
   C with a peace treaty
   D with the death of one of the
      rebellion's leaders

11. What inspired the Great Migration?
   A the establishment of religious
      freedom throughout the colonies
   B the start of civil war in Great
      Britain
   C the success of the Plymouth and
      Massachusetts Bay colonies
   D the establishment of peace between
      Native Americans and settlers

12. Why did Roger Williams establish the
    colony of Rhode Island?
   A He received a land grant.
   B He believed that church and state
      should be separate.
   C He wanted to create a more
      democratic government.
   D He wanted to make a profit.

13. How did the witch scare in Salem end?
   A The witch trials were condemned,
      and the remaining prisoners were
      freed.
   B The hysteria slowly died down,
      although fear of witches continued
      to dominate life in New England.
   C Strict laws were passed to prevent
      future instances of witchcraft.
   D The witch trials were declared a
      success because all of the witches
      had been executed.

14. How did proprietary colonies differ
    from joint-stock colonies?
   A They were established by investors
      hoping to make a profit.
   B They were strictly religious.
   C They were under the direct control
      of the king of England.
   D They were founded by private
      individuals.

15. The Pilgrims that traveled on the
    Mayflower established which
    settlement?
   A Jamestown Colony
   B Plymouth Colony
   C Massachusetts Bay Colony
   D Rhode Island Colony

16. Why were Quakers jailed and
    persecuted in England?
   A They supported a rigid class
      structure.
   B They were pacifists who refused to
      fight in wars.
   C They called for a return to
      Catholicism.
   D They wanted to take control of the
      English government.

17. Why was the colony of Georgia
    established?
   A to serve as a military "buffer zone"
      between the Carolinas and Spanish
      Florida
   B to create a refuge for Catholics
   C to make a profit for the trustees of
      the colony
   D to create a democracy

18. **Narrative Writing** Write a short story
    about an English colonist who has just
    arrived in Jamestown. Include specific
    challenges that the main character
    faces.

Colonial Life

Test Preparation

DIRECTIONS Read each question and circle the letter of the best response.

1. What was one result of the Navigation Acts?
   A English involvement in colonial affairs decreased.
   B Certain colonial industries, such as lumber and shipbuilding, declined.
   C Resentment of these laws led many colonists to sabotage English shipping.
   D British revenues increased, but the costs of law enforcement in America also increased.

2. According to the principles of mercantilism, a nation's power was directly related to which of the following?
   A its wealth
   B its political system
   C the extent of its empire
   D the strength of its military

3. Why was the English Bill of Rights a significant document?
   A It was the world's first written constitution.
   B It gave Parliament many powers over the monarchy.
   C It abolished slavery throughout the English empire.
   D It gave women the right to vote.

4. How did the Glorious Revolution affect the colonies?
   A The monarchy strengthened its rule over the colonies.
   B It led to several small uprisings.
   C Colonists largely ignored the revolution because it did not apply to them.
   D It led to the creation of the Dominion of New England.

5. Why was the Board of Trade established?
   A to regulate trade between England and the colonies
   B to ensure that the Navigation Acts were enforced
   C to help the colonists move toward self-government
   D to handle colonial affairs

6. How did Sir Edmund Andros infuriate the colonists?
   A by prohibiting Anglican services
   B by imposing new taxes
   C by calling for elected assemblies
   D by passing the Navigation Acts

7. What is the name for the horrific journey that enslaved Africans made across the Atlantic Ocean?
   A the Middle Passage
   B triangular trade
   C the Atlantic Passage
   D the Great Awakening

8. What was one result of the Great Awakening?
   A a decrease in unity among the colonists
   B the creation of several respected centers of learning
   C the growth of Catholicism in America
   D a decrease in church membership in the 1700s

9. What was America's most valuable export?
   A indigo
   B cotton
   C tobacco
   D rice

Test Preparation

Colonial Life Test Preparation

10. For early colonists, where did North America's most valuable resources come from?
    A the plentiful fresh water
    B the thick forests
    C the mineral-rich soil
    D the ocean

11. Which Enlightenment thinker believed that it was the duty of government to protect the citizens' natural rights?
    A Baron de Montesquieu
    B Jean-Jacques Rousseau
    C Sir Isaac Newton
    D John Locke

12. Jonathan Edwards was a part of what religious movement?
    A the Enlightenment
    B the Glorious Revolution
    C the Great Awakening
    D the Reformation

13. Who won the first important victory for freedom of the press in the American colonies?
    A Benjamin Franklin
    B George Whitefield
    C John Peter Zenger
    D Eliza Lucas

14. Who revolted in the Stono Rebellion?
    A indentured servants
    B enslaved Africans
    C Native Americans
    D yeoman farmers

15. The Iroquois League allied itself with which of the following?
    A France
    B Great Britain
    C Spain
    D the colonies

16. Which of the following was true of the African American community?
    A Kinship networks helped look after those who had lost families.
    B Most African Americans rejected their traditional African beliefs in favor of Christianity.
    C The Enlightenment inspired many African Americans to seek their freedom.
    D The difficult nature of their lives prevented African Americans from developing their own culture.

17. What was the purpose of the Proclamation of 1763?
    A to prevent the colonists from taking French lands
    B to reserve the fur trade as a British industry
    C to unite the colonies
    D to avoid conflicts with Native Americans

18. Which of the following was a result of the French and Indian War?
    A Britain gained control of the entire continent.
    B France gained control over the northern British colonies.
    C Britain gained all French land east of the Mississippi River.
    D Britain received the territory of Louisiana.

19. **Persuasive Writing** If you were living in a southern colony, how would you convince a friend to move to your colony? Write a letter to your friend.

The Revolutionary Era   ## Test Preparation

DIRECTIONS Read each question and circle the letter of the best response.

1. How did the French and Indian War affect the colonists?
   A The colonists sold many goods to the armies and benefited.
   B Because the French lost the war, they had to pay the colonists.
   C The war left Britain with an army of 10,000 in the colonies.
   D The war left the colonists with a huge debt.

2. When Samuel Adams protested "taxation without representation," what was his major complaint?
   A The colonists could not raise taxes to build roads.
   B The colonists did not have a representative in Parliament.
   C The colonists could not travel west of the Appalachian Mountains.
   D The colonists were tired of quartering British soldiers.

3. Rising tensions between the British and colonists was seen in what 1770 event?
   A the passage of the Intolerable Acts
   B the battle of Lexington
   C the passage of the Stamp Act
   D the Boston Massacre

4. What were two results of the First Continental Congress?
   A boycotts of British goods and a force of minutemen
   B a truce with Britain and increased trade
   C boycotts of British goods and a declaration of war
   D a constitution establishing basic human rights and increased trade

5. Where were the first shots fired in the Revolutionary War?
   A Boston
   B New York
   C Lexington and Concord
   D Virginia

6. The Second Continental Congress met in 1775 and created what group?
   A the Continental Army
   B the minutemen
   C the Committees of Correspondence
   D the Sons of Liberty

7. What 50-page pamphlet sold more than 100,000 copies?
   A the Declaration of Independence
   B the Olive Branch Petition
   C *Common Sense*
   D *Two Treatises of Government*

8. What was the name for colonists who supported Britain?
   A Patriots
   B Loyalists
   C minutemen
   D delegates

9. Who pressured the drafters of the Declaration of Independence to cut out a section condemning slavery?
   A Samuel Adams
   B Loyalists
   C New England colonists
   D southern colonists

10. Was the Battle of Bunker Hill a victory or a defeat for the colonists?
    A Despite a retreat, it was a public relations victory.
    B It was an outright victory.
    C It was an outright defeat.
    D Despite a victory, it was a public relations defeat.

The Revolutionary Era   # Test Preparation

11. Look at the chart below. Use your knowledge of history to answer the following question.

The Continental Army
Strengths   • Strong military leadership   • Soldiers fighting for a cause they believed in   • Fighting on home territory
Weaknesses   • Small, untrained military   • Shortages of resources   • Weak central government

What were one strength and one weakness of the British Army?

A strength: well-trained military; weakness: fighting in familiar land

B strength: ample resources; weakness: weak central government

C strength: well-trained military; weakness: fighting far from home

D strength: alliance with France; weakness: alliance with Loyalists

12. What is one example of how the British followed traditional European methods of warfare?

A They only fought during daylight.

B They did not fight during winter.

C They only fought using cannons.

D They did not wear uniforms.

13. The turning point in the Revolutionary War is thought to have occurred where?

A the Battle of Saratoga

B the Battle of Yorktown

C the Battle of Trenton

D the Battle of Bunker Hill

14. What is one reason that France helped the colonists during the Revolutionary War?

A France wanted control of the colonies.

B France wanted to attack Spain in the South.

C France wanted to find gold in America.

D France wanted to restore its power in Europe.

15. Where did British troops finally surrender?

A New York

B Yorktown

C Saratoga

D King's Mountain

16. What document ended the Revolutionary War and included Britain's official recognition of the United States?

A Treaty of Paris

B Declaration of Independence

C *Common Sense*

D Proclamation of 1763

17. After the war, what happened to the relationship between churches and governments?

A They grew closer together.

B They became more separate.

C Churches became the official national government.

D The national government outlawed churches.

18. **Narrative Writing** Write several journal entries that a shopkeeper might have written in the early days of the war. Be sure to include his or her feelings about committing to the fight. Use specific details to add interest.

Creating a New Government

Test Preparation

DIRECTIONS Read each question and circle the letter of the best response.

1. Even though the states differed in many ways, they all shared what feature of government?
   A the same laws concerning trade
   B a common currency
   C the institution of slavery
   D three branches of government

2. After the war, Americans wanted what kind of government?
   A monarchy
   B republic
   C joint-stock company
   D no government at all

3. What were the Articles of Confederation?
   A the nation's first constitution
   B the peace treaty with Britain
   C the plan for settling the West
   D the agreement signed with Native Americans

4. What was one of the weaknesses of the Articles of Confederation?
   A Congress could not declare war.
   B Congress could not pass laws.
   C Congress could not collect taxes.
   D Congress could not open new land to settlement.

5. Why were the British able to occupy territory that the United States had won in the 1783 Treaty of Paris?
   A The American government was too weak to remove them.
   B The American government welcomed their presence.
   C Native American groups defended them against American attack.
   D The British and the Americans signed a new treaty.

6. Look at the map below. Use your knowledge of history to answer the following question.

Why do you think Ohio's date of statehood is so much earlier than Wisconsin's?
   A The people of Wisconsin were less interested in statehood.
   B The state of Wisconsin had to meet different standards for statehood.
   C People settled in Ohio faster than Wisconsin.
   D Wisconsin lost some of its population to Canada.

7. What divided the Northwest Territory into a grid of townships?
   A Native Americans
   B the Land Ordinance of 1785
   C the Articles of Confederation
   D settlers

8. What led to the Constitutional Convention in 1787?
   A the continued practice of slavery
   B the threat of war with France
   C frustration over the Articles of Confederation
   D an agreement with Native Americans

Creating a New Government   Test Preparation

9. What was one of the biggest challenges at the Constitutional Convention?
   A fighting for the right to declare war
   B giving women the right to vote
   C figuring out how to outlaw slavery
   D finding a balance between large and small states

10. What was the name for giving each branch of government power over the other two branches?
   A the Great Compromise
   B checks and balances
   C the Three-Fifths Compromise
   D bicameral legislature

11. Which of the following is an example of a power the legislative branch has over the executive?
   A It can appoint judges.
   B It can veto bills.
   C It can interpret laws.
   D It can reject treaties.

12. What were Alexander Hamilton's feelings about the national government?
   A He favored a strong central government.
   B He favored a weak central government.
   C He thought the economy would benefit from a weak government.
   D He thought a strong central government was bad for farmers.

13. What was the name for those who distrusted a strong central government?
   A Antifederalists
   B Federalists
   C Royalists
   D Republicans

14. What was added to the Constitution to gain the approval of Antifederalists?
   A the right to vote for all men
   B the outlaw of slavery
   C the Bill of Rights
   D the promise of no taxes

15. Where could people read a strong defense of the new constitution?
   A *The Federalist*
   B *Common Sense*
   C the Bill of Rights
   D *Two Treatises on Government*

16. How many states needed to ratify the Constitution for it to take effect?
   A seven
   B nine
   C eleven
   D all of them

17. Which rights were most protected by the Bill of Rights?
   A the rights of the government
   B the rights of individuals
   C the rights of business owners
   D the rights of women

18. Why would states be happy about the Tenth Amendment and its definition of reserved powers?
   A It said that states held a majority of governmental powers.
   B It said the federal government would take care of everything.
   C It said states could do whatever they wanted.
   D It gave more power to the states.

19. **Persuasive Writing** Write a letter to a friend to convince him or her either to support or not support the ratification of the Constitution. Support your argument with facts.

Forging the New Republic   Test Preparation

DIRECTIONS Read each question and circle the letter of the best response.

1. What was the name for the group of people that ran George Washington's executive departments?
   A the Whiskey Rebellion
   B the cabinet
   C political parties
   D the National Bank

2. Where was the nation's capital when Washington was inaugurated?
   A New York City
   B Philadelphia
   C Washington, D.C.
   D Boston

3. What laid out the plan for the judicial branch of government?
   A the Constitution
   B the Articles of Confederation
   C the political parties
   D the Judiciary Act of 1789

4. What was one of Alexander Hamilton's measures for raising money for the government?
   A moving the national capital
   B the Tariff of 1789
   C establishing a Department of Treasury
   D the Judiciary Act of 1789

5. What is the best way to summarize the attitudes of those that favored strict construction?
   A Tariffs are bad because they make imported goods more expensive.
   B Political parties are bad because they will divide the nation.
   C The government can only do what the Constitution states it can do.
   D Repaying bonds at face value is unfair to the original bondholders.

6. The deep split in how leaders viewed the role of government led to what political event?
   A the creation of the National Bank
   B the formation of political parties
   C a civil war
   D the Whiskey Rebellion

7. How did George Washington react to war in Europe?
   A He pledged support to Britain.
   B He pledged support to France.
   C He said the nation would remain neutral.
   D He said the nation would sell arms to all European powers.

8. What did the Miamis do after losing the Battle of Fallen Timbers?
   A signed the Treaty of Greenville, giving up much of their land
   B made alliances with other native groups to continue fighting
   C joined forces with the French to attack the Northwest Territory
   D applied for statehood under the Northwest Ordinance of 1787

9. What was the effect of the XYZ Affair on public opinion?
   A Americans were insulted and angry with France.
   B Americans were scared of getting involved in a European war.
   C Americans were in favor of neutrality in all foreign affairs.
   D Americans called for war against Britain.

10. What was the name of the effort to limit free speech in 1789?
    A the XYZ Affair
    B Jay's Treaty
    C the Sedition Act
    D sectionalism

Forging the New Republic   Test Preparation

11. Who won the bitter election of 1800?
    A John Adams
    B Thomas Jefferson
    C Aaron Burr
    D James Madison

12. What was Thomas Jefferson's greatest diplomatic victory?
    A joining the revolution in France
    B defeating the English navy
    C acquiring the Louisiana Purchase
    D achieving peace between Britain and France

13. What was the government's best-known attempt to explore the newly enlarged country?
    A the XYZ Affair
    B the Lewis and Clark expedition
    C the Twelfth Amendment
    D judicial review

14. What caused the famous court case *Marbury* v. *Madison*?
    A the acquisition of new land by Thomas Jefferson's government
    B the contested election of 1800
    C the question over the National Bank
    D the Federalist effort to pack the judiciary with their judges

15. What is the best way to summarize the power of judicial review?
    A The government has the power to interpret the Constitution.
    B The Supreme Court has the power to declare laws unconstitutional.
    C Congress has the power to pass legislation.
    D The Supreme Court has the power to impeach the president.

16. What was one of Thomas Jefferson's failures as president?
    A impressment
    B judicial review
    C the Embargo Act
    D the Louisiana Purchase

17. What was the cause of the Battle of Tippecanoe?
    A the British policy of impressment
    B tension between Native Americans and the American army
    C the policies of Napoleon
    D tension between Spanish forces in the South and the American army

18. Why did more calls for war against Britain come from the frontier states than from anywhere else?
    A They were more anti-British than anyone else.
    B They were more concerned with world events than anyone else.
    C They were tired of competing with British manufactured goods.
    D They knew they could defeat the British with Indian help.

19. What document ended the War of 1812?
    A the Treaty of Paris
    B Jay's Treaty
    C the Treaty of Ghent
    D the Alien Act

20. **Expository Writing** Write a short essay explaining how the Louisiana Purchase was both a good thing and a huge challenge for the new nation. Be sure to use specific examples to illustrate your point.

From Nationalism to Sectionalism

Test Preparation

DIRECTIONS Read each question and circle the letter of the best response.

1. James Fenimore Cooper and Washington Irving were essential in establishing what part of the new American culture?
   A painting
   B literature
   C music
   D sculpture

2. Which of the following was part of the domestic policy called the American System?
   A guaranteeing all children a public school education
   B expanding the nation through warfare
   C giving women the right to vote
   D passing a tariff to protect American manufacturing

3. Which of the following best summarizes the message of the Monroe Doctrine?
   A European powers should not attempt to colonize lands in the Americas any further.
   B European powers are welcome to invest in the Americas.
   C European powers should no longer send ships to U.S. ports.
   D European powers are welcome to establish governments in South America.

4. Which 1820 agreement dealt with the number of slave and free states?
   A the Monroe Doctrine
   B the Missouri Compromise
   C the American System
   D the Adams-Onís Treaty

5. Use this table to answer the following question.

Heavy Toll on the Five Tribes		
	People Removed	Lives Lost
Cherokee	18,000	4,500
Choctaw	14,000	3,500
Creek	15,000	3,500
Chickasaw	4,000	unknown
Seminole	4,000	unknown

About how many Cherokees died during their removal?
   A 3,500
   B 4,000
   C 4,500
   D unknown

6. Who created the Democratic Party?
   A Daniel Webster and his supporters
   B John Quincy Adams and his supporters
   C Andrew Jackson and his supporters
   D Henry Clay and his supporters

7. What was the Indian Removal Act?
   A a law moving Native Americans from their homes in the Southeast to a new territory in the West
   B a law removing whites from Native American lands
   C a law moving Native Americans to nicer homes in eastern cities
   D a law removing immigrants from Native American lands

8. Which Native American group used armed force to resist the U.S. Army?
   A the Cherokee
   B the Seminole
   C the Creek
   D the Chickasaw

From Nationalism to Sectionalism

Test Preparation

9. Why did Andrew Jackson want to eliminate the Second Bank of the United States?
   A He thought businesses should borrow money directly from the government instead.
   B He thought the bank supported Native American groups.
   C He thought people should not keep their money in banks.
   D He thought the bank favored the rich over the poor.

10. What was the central issue in the nullification crisis?
   A Indian removal
   B tariffs
   C slavery
   D national banks

11. What was the first industry to be affected by the Industrial Revolution?
   A the textile industry
   B the shipbuilding industry
   C the transportation industry
   D the weapons industry

12. What invention connected Americans like no other before it?
   A cotton gin
   B telegraph
   C canal
   D steam engine

13. What did Robert Fulton create on the Hudson River in 1807?
   A the largest textile mill in New England
   B the longest bridge connecting New York to New Jersey
   C the first steamboat service for passengers
   D the fastest printing press in New York

14. The fight over the Second Bank of the United States was essentially a fight over what?
   A states' rights
   B Indian removal
   C national expansion
   D tariffs

15. Where was the Cotton Belt located?
   A the North
   B the West
   C the South
   D the Northwest

16. How many of the white families in the South owned slaves?
   A one-fourth
   B one-third
   C one-half
   D two-thirds

17. As trade and industry grew, what happened to cities?
   A They shrank.
   B They were replaced with farms.
   C They grew in size.
   D They failed to be profitable.

18. How many enslaved African Americans were there in the United States by 1840?
   A 25,000
   B 250,000
   C 2,500,000
   D 25,000,000

19. **Expository Writing** Write a brief essay describing how the North differed from the South in the year 1840.

A Push for Reform

Test Preparation

DIRECTIONS Read each question and circle the letter of the best response.

1. What was the name for the religious movement that swept the country in the 1820s and 1830s?
   A the temperance movement
   B the transcendentalist movement
   C the Second Great Awakening
   D the First Great Awakening

2. What was the main goal of the temperance movement?
   A to promote religion
   B to reduce the use of alcoholic beverages
   C to reform prisons
   D to reform common schools

3. Who was the best-known advocate of school reform?
   A Dorothea Dix
   B Horace Mann
   C Henry David Thoreau
   D Charles Grandison Finney

4. Which of the following was a transcendentalist belief?
   A Knowledge is only found through observation of the world.
   B People should depend on one another and accept traditional beliefs.
   C All people and all of nature are connected.
   D People should not be involved in social reform.

5. Creating perfect communities was a goal of which movement?
   A the prison reform movement
   B the utopian movement
   C the transcendentalist movement
   D the common-school movement

6. Who was one of the best-known transcendentalists and the author of *Walden*?
   A Horace Mann
   B Ralph Waldo Emerson
   C Dorothea Dix
   D Henry David Thoreau

7. What drove many Irish immigrants to the United States?
   A the Great Irish Famine
   B the Know-Nothings
   C the labor movement
   D the temperance movement

8. Which of the following is a reason Irish immigrants were treated poorly?
   A their skillfulness in farming
   B their history of attacking America
   C their poverty and willingness to work for low wages
   D their skin color

9. Which of the following groups could be described as nativist?
   A Irish immigrants
   B German immigrants
   C Know-Nothings
   D temperance reformers

10. What were the major differences between most Irish and German immigrants?
   A Irish were poor and Catholic while Germans were middle class and Protestant.
   B Irish were middle class and Protestant while Germans were poor and Catholic.
   C Irish were middle class and Catholic while Germans were poor and Protestant.
   D Irish were poor and Protestant while Germans were middle class and Catholic.

A Push for Reform

Test Preparation

11. How did immigration to the United States in the middle 1800s affect city life?
    A It led to a more equal distribution of wealth.
    B It led to the growth of slavery.
    C It led to urbanization.
    D It ended the reform movements.

12. Which of the following was a right of most women in the early 1800s?
    A the right to own property
    B the right to marry
    C the right to vote
    D the right to hold public office

13. The view that "a woman's place is in the home" is an example of what kind of limit?
    A an economic limit
    B a legal limit
    C a political limit
    D a cultural limit

14. What is the best way to describe the Seneca Falls Convention?
    A the first women's rights convention in America
    B the first meeting of women against political reform
    C the first convention on school reform
    D the first meeting of the Second Great Awakening

15. Where did most enslaved people live?
    A in cities
    B on farms or plantations in the South
    C on farms or plantations in the North
    D in the West

16. How were enslaved African Americans viewed under the law?
    A as citizens, with full rights
    B as foreigners, with limited rights
    C as a labor force, with partial rights
    D as property, with no rights

17. What was the Underground Railroad?
    A a system of buried telegraph lines
    B a rail line between New York and Virginia
    C a secret, informal system of escape routes for slaves
    D a train that ran to the North

18. What was Nat Turner's most famous feat?
    A becoming the first free black mayor in the South
    B leading a slave revolt
    C owning a large plantation in Virginia
    D escaping to the North and starting a newspaper

19. Who published the first abolitionist newspaper?
    A William Lloyd Garrison
    B Sarah and Angelina Grimké
    C Elihu Embree
    D Frederick Douglass

20. **Narrative Writing** Write a description of what it might have been like to travel from Virginia to Pennsylvania as a slave on the Underground Railroad. Include both factual details of the experience and emotions one might have felt.

Expansion Leads to Conflict

Test Preparation

DIRECTIONS Read each question and circle the letter of the best response.

1. What was the name for the idea that Americans had a God-given right to all of North America?
   A the Enlightenment
   B sectionalism
   C gold rush
   D manifest destiny

2. What was the longest and most famous trail migrants used to travel west?
   A the Santa Fe Trail
   B the Oregon Trail
   C the Mormon Trail
   D the California Trail

3. What was one reason Mormons wanted to resettle in the West?
   A They often faced persecution where they lived.
   B They wanted to own more slaves.
   C Many of them were gold miners.
   D They wanted to convert Native Americans.

4. What important discovery was made in California in 1848?
   A oil
   B gold
   C dinosaur bones
   D electricity

5. Which trail was used by migrants seeking gold on the West Coast?
   A the Mormon Trail
   B the Oregon Trail
   C the California Trail
   D the Santa Fe Trail

6. The slogan "Fifty-four Forty or Fight!" referred to the boundary of which area?
   A Oregon
   B California
   C Utah
   D Missouri

7. Why were the Butterfield Trail and the Pony Express important?
   A They were the first railroad lines in the country.
   B They carried settlers and their belongings over long distances.
   C They allowed Americans to communicate with each other.
   D They were the fastest way to move a religious group to the West.

8. Who had previously settled in Texas before Americans?
   A Native Americans and the Spanish
   B Mormons and the Spanish
   C New Englanders and the British
   D Native Americans and the British

9. What was the first European method used to govern Texas?
   A manifest destiny
   B mission system
   C gold rush
   D plantation system

10. Why was the Spanish attempt to convert the original population of Texas to Christianity unsuccessful?
   A The Spanish were more interested in finding gold than converting Native Americans.
   B Americans took over the efforts to convert Native Americans.
   C Native Americans had already been converted to Christianity.
   D Most Native Americans did not want to give up their religion.

Expansion Leads to Conflict   Test Preparation

---

11. The Texas Venture involved an agreement between which two parties?
    A the Mexican government and the U.S. government
    B an American settler and the Mexican government
    C the Spanish government and the U.S. government
    D an American settler and the Spanish government

12. American settlers won control over the Mexican territory of Texas after which conflict?
    A the War of 1812
    B the Texas Revolution
    C the Mexican-American War
    D the Civil War

13. After Mexico had to withdraw its troops from Texas, what became of the territory?
    A It immediately became a U.S. state called Texas.
    B It became an independent state within Mexico.
    C It became an independent nation called the Republic of Texas.
    D It became a U.S. territory.

14. Why were some northerners hesitant to annex Texas as a state?
    A It was a slave state.
    B It was a Mormon state.
    C It was a free state.
    D It was full of Americans.

15. What event prompted Mexico to cut off its diplomatic relations with the United States?
    A the U.S. annexation of Texas
    B the Texas Revolution
    C the Civil War
    D the gold rush

16. Read this quote from President James K. Polk. Use your understanding of history to answer the question below.

> To enlarge [the United States] is to extend the dominions of peace over additional territories and increasing millions . . . my duty [is] to assert and maintain . . . the right of the United States to that portion of our territory which lies beyond the Rocky Mountains.

Why would the government of Mexico have been upset over these words?
    A Mexico had a personal feud with Polk.
    B Mexico supported the independence of the Republic of Texas.
    C Mexico owned the lands that Polk was referring to.
    D Mexico wanted to acquire those lands for itself.

17. How did the United States benefit from the Treaty of Guadalupe Hidalgo?
    A It settled the border dispute, but no land was exchanged.
    B It gained a huge piece of land in the West.
    C It was able to outlaw slavery in Texas.
    D It now controlled all Mexican land north of Mexico City.

18. **Persuasive Writing** If you were a farmer in Texas in the year 1840, how would you convince your friend back East that Texas needs to be part of the Union? Write a letter to your friend.

The Nation Splits Apart   Test Preparation

DIRECTIONS Read each question and circle the letter of the best response.

1. Why was California's application for statehood controversial?
   A It could lead to war with Mexico.
   B It would be the largest state.
   C It would tip the balance between free and slave states.
   D It would be costly.

2. Which of the following was a provision of the Fugitive Slave Act?
   A Escaped slaves that had lived in the North for years could be captured and returned to slavery.
   B Slavery would be legal in all states.
   C Escaped slaves that made it to the North would become free.
   D Slavery would be illegal in all states.

3. What was another name for letting voters decide for themselves whether their state should be a slave or a free state?
   A compromise
   B abolition
   C nativism
   D popular sovereignty

4. Which of the following ended the Missouri Compromise's limits on slavery?
   A the Compromise of 1850
   B the Kansas-Nebraska Act
   C the Fugitive Slave Act
   D the annexation of California

5. Who wrote the best-seller *Uncle Tom's Cabin*?
   A Henry Clay
   B Millard Fillmore
   C Harriet Beecher Stowe
   D Daniel Webster

6. What party was formed in 1854 to oppose slavery?
   A the Republican Party
   B the Democratic Party
   C the Free-Soil Party
   D the Liberty Party

7. Why was the Kansas Territory called "Bleeding Kansas" in 1856?
   A There was violence between pro-slavery and antislavery groups.
   B Kansas was losing population to Missouri.
   C Hospitals were closed in Kansas due to a lack of funds.
   D Native American groups were making frequent attacks.

8. Which abolitionist led the Pottawatomie Massacre?
   A James Buchanan
   B John Brown
   C Dred Scott
   D Charles Sumner

9. How did the Supreme Court rule in the *Dred Scott* case?
   A The Missouri Compromise was unconstitutional.
   B Popular sovereignty was the only legal way to settle the slavery debate.
   C The Fugitive Slave Act was unconstitutional.
   D The Constitution protected slaveholding as a property right.

10. The Lecompton Constitution was submitted in which state?
   A Nebraska
   B Kansas
   C Missouri
   D Texas

The Nation Splits Apart   Test Preparation

---

11. Who led the plot to start a slave rebellion in Virginia?
    A Dred Scott
    B Frederick Douglas
    C Harriet Beecher Stowe
    D John Brown

12. What was the result of the raid on Harpers Ferry?
    A A slave revolt established a free zone in northern Virginia.
    B A slave revolt never began, and the leaders were captured and hanged.
    C Congress pardoned the leaders and reconsidered its position on slavery.
    D Slave revolts occurred all over the South.

13. What were Abraham Lincoln's early feelings about slavery?
    A He thought it was wrong.
    B He thought it was acceptable.
    C He had no sympathy for slaves.
    D He thought Congress should immediately abolish slavery.

14. The Lincoln-Douglas debates took place during which political event?
    A the campaign for the Illinois U.S. Senate seat
    B James Buchanan's inauguration
    C the campaign for the presidency of the United States
    D the congressional debate over the Kansas-Nebraska Act

15. Which of the following was a result of the Lincoln-Douglas debates?
    A southern Democrats supported Lincoln
    B many slave revolts
    C national exposure for Lincoln
    D the abolition of slavery

16. Which of the following was a reason Abraham Lincoln won the election of 1860?
    A The nation was solidly antislavery.
    B Four candidates split the vote, and Lincoln came out with the most.
    C The nation was solidly pro-slavery.
    D Lincoln was by far the most popular candidate in the South.

17. What did South Carolina's legislature do one week after Abraham Lincoln won the presidential election?
    A It called a convention to consider withdrawing from the Union.
    B It passed a resolution saying it regretted the election results.
    C It declared war on northern, antislavery states.
    D It promised to abolish slavery over time.

18. What did most southern states do three months after Lincoln's victory?
    A set up a series of meetings with northern leaders to negotiate a secession agreement
    B held a religious meeting to pray for the Union
    C established the Confederate States of America
    D held a series of debates over whether slavery was necessary

19. **Narrative Writing** Write a short story describing what it might have felt like to live in a southern state immediately after the presidential election of 1860. Include historical facts as well as the main character's feelings about the event.

The Civil War

Test Preparation

DIRECTIONS Read each question and circle the letter of the best response.

1. Where were the first shots of the Civil War fired?
   A Washington, D.C.
   B New York City
   C Atlanta
   D Charleston

2. Maryland, Kentucky, and Missouri were examples of what?
   A Confederate states
   B border states
   C Union states
   D neutral states

3. Which of the following was a major advantage for the South?
   A It was more populous.
   B It had many of the nation's most talented army officers.
   C It had the support of Great Britain.
   D It had a superior industrial system.

4. Which of the following was a major advantage for the North?
   A It could fight a defensive war.
   B It was fighting for abolition.
   C It was more populous.
   D Its population believed they were fighting for their freedom and their homeland.

5. Why did southerners think the British would come to their aid?
   A They thought that Britain would want revenge for the War of 1812.
   B They thought that Britain would want cotton badly enough to fight for the South.
   C They thought that Britain supported their tradition of slavery.
   D They thought that Britain preferred southern manufactured goods to northern goods.

6. What was the result of the first major battle of the Civil War, the First Battle of Bull Run?
   A a clear victory for the South
   B a clear victory for the North
   C there was no clear winner
   D the battle was canceled due to civilians getting in the way

7. Which of the following best describes cavalry?
   A a line of infantrymen
   B a row of cannons
   C observation balloons
   D soldiers on horseback

8. Which of the following was used to move large numbers of troops for the first time in the Civil War?
   A balloons
   B steamboats
   C large wagons
   D railroads

9. Which of the following were critical to the North's campaign in the Mississippi River Valley?
   A caravels
   B ironclads
   C steamboats
   D cavalry

10. In which battle did the bloodiest day of the Civil War occur?
    A the First Battle of Bull Run
    B the Battle of Shiloh
    C the Battle of Antietam
    D the Battle of Vicksburg

11. Which general led his troops to victory in the Battle of Chancellorsville?
    A Ulysses S. Grant
    B Robert E. Lee
    C George McClellan
    D George Meade

The Civil War

Test Preparation

12. What was the impact of the Emancipation Proclamation?
    A All slaves in the United States were freed.
    B Riots broke out.
    C Great Britain refused to intervene in the war on the behalf of the South.
    D African Americans were allowed to fight in units with white soldiers.

13. What was the Union response to hearing about the horrible conditions at the Confederate Andersonville prison camp?
    A limiting Confederate prisoners' food to only bread and water
    B negotiating a complete prisoner exchange
    C establishing a strict code of prisoners' rights
    D attacking Andersonville and liberating the Union prisoners

14. What did the Confederate Congress implement when it became concerned about maintaining its army?
    A the nation's first military draft
    B improved pay and benefits for its soldiers
    C family visits
    D the nation's first comprehensive health care system

15. For which of the following is Clara Barton remembered?
    A becoming the first woman to hold a federal government job
    B serving as a Union spy
    C founding the American Red Cross
    D disguising herself as a man and enlisting in the army

16. What was California's greatest contribution to the war?
    A troops
    B gold
    C weapons
    D military leaders

17. Which battle secured the West for the Union?
    A Battle of Chickamauga
    B Battle of Pea Ridge
    C Battle of Glorieta Pass
    D Battle of Chancellorsville

18. How were Republicans able to abolish slavery in the United States?
    A by passing the Thirteenth Amendment in Congress
    B by freeing slaves from every plantation in the South
    C by convincing the Confederacy to end the practice
    D by having Abraham Lincoln give a speech announcing the end of slavery

19. Roughly how many people died in the Civil War?
    A 6,000
    B 60,000
    C 600,000
    D 6,000,000

20. **Expository Writing** Write a short essay explaining the different advantages held by the North and the South and how they related to the outcome of the war. Include specific facts and details.

Reconstruction

Test Preparation

DIRECTIONS Read each question and circle the letter of the best response.

1. Which of the following was a practical concern for African Americans living in the South after the war?
   A obtaining their freedom
   B obtaining a job
   C relocating to the West
   D gaining experience in factories

2. The Reconstruction Acts achieved which of the following?
   A forced former Confederate officers to serve time in prison
   B divided the South into five military districts
   C provided free farms to African Americans
   D put African Americans into public office

3. What was the purpose of the Freedmen's Bureau?
   A to build up the Union Army with southerners in need of jobs
   B to roam the countryside making sure all slaves were freed
   C to own and operate every southern plantation
   D to provide assistance to black and white southerners who had been uprooted by the war

4. Why did some members of Congress oppose Abraham Lincoln's plan for Reconstruction?
   A They believed southern states did not need to be readmitted to the Union.
   B They thought it was too lenient.
   C They wanted southern states to create their own governments.
   D They wanted to be more forgiving toward high-ranking Confederate leaders.

5. Study the graph below and answer the following question.

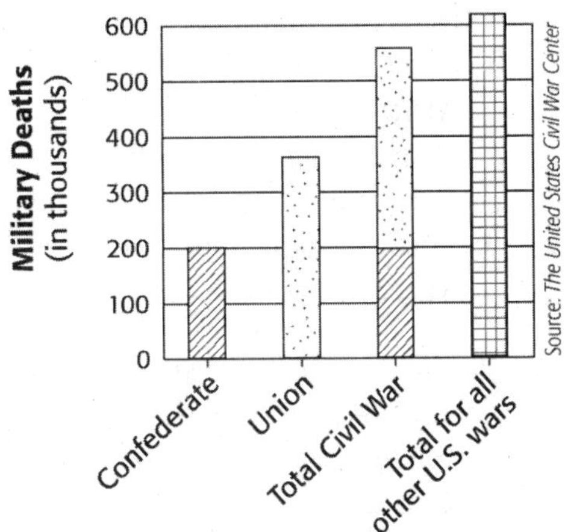

Note: Total deaths for all other U.S. wars is limited to deaths through the Gulf War.

Approximately how many Union soldiers were killed in the war?
   A 250,000
   B 350,000
   C 450,000
   D 550,000

6. Who was responsible for the assassination of President Abraham Lincoln?
   A Confederate conspirators trying to overthrow the government
   B Union soldiers unhappy with the long war
   C Confederate soldiers who attacked Lincoln in battle
   D Draft rioters unhappy with forced service in the army

7. Which southern laws were designed to keep freedmen in a slavelike condition?
   A Labor Codes
   B Johnson Laws
   C Black Codes
   D Johnson Codes

                                                            Test Preparation

Reconstruction

Test Preparation

8. Which of the following best describes the Ku Klux Klan?
   A an organization that helped freedmen find jobs
   B a church group that preached to African Americans
   C a government agency that discriminated against freedmen
   D a private social club that terrorized African Americans

9. Who took over Reconstruction from President Andrew Johnson?
   A freedmen
   B Radical Republicans
   C the Ku Klux Klan
   D southern Democrats

10. Which amendment gave citizenship to all people born in the United States?
    A Thirteenth Amendment
    B Fourteenth Amendment
    C Fifteenth Amendment
    D Sixteenth Amendment

11. Which amendment stated that no one could be denied the right to vote due to race?
    A Thirteenth Amendment
    B Fourteenth Amendment
    C Fifteenth Amendment
    D Sixteenth Amendment

12. The Enforcement Acts empowered the army and federal court to punish which of the following groups?
    A Radical Republicans
    B the Ku Klux Klan
    C the Redeemers
    D carpetbaggers

13. Study the table below and answer the following question.

Hopes Raised and Denied

Freedom	Rights Denied
• Slavery banned	• Sharecropping system created cycle of debt
• Free to work for wages	• Ability to vote and hold office restricted
• Could move and live anywhere	• White leadership regained control of southern state governments
• Many families reunited	
• Could serve in political office	

Which of the following is a reason that freedmen had their rights denied?
   A They were not interested in holding public office.
   B They were constantly attacking their former owners.
   C They did not own land and were powerless.
   D They were not interested in economic or political power.

14. How did landowners benefit from sharecropping?
    A They did not have to pay their workers.
    B They did not have to provide supplies to their workers.
    C Workers had to choose which crop to grow.
    D They could supervise groups of workers.

15. **Expository Writing** Write a brief essay describing the debate in Washington, D.C., over Reconstruction. Explain the attitudes of each side, as well as its goals.

The American West   Test Preparation

DIRECTIONS Read each question and circle the letter of the best response.

1. Which of the following threatened the way of life of the Plains Indians?
   A the institution of slavery
   B the disappearance of the buffalo
   C the Civil War
   D attacks from other Native American groups

2. Why did some Americans see the Ghost Dance as a threat?
   A They were opposed to any kind of dancing for religious reasons.
   B They wanted all Native Americans to convert to Christianity.
   C They saw it as the beginnings of an uprising by Native Americans.
   D They thought it might give political power to Native Americans.

3. What battle upset the U.S. Army and strengthened its commitment to removing the Indian threat to western settlers?
   A Battle of the Little Bighorn
   B Sand Creek Massacre
   C Wounded Knee Massacre
   D Battle of Palo Duro Canyon

4. What government agency was in charge of the policy of Americanization of Native American groups?
   A the U.S. Army
   B the Department of Treasury
   C the Bureau of Indian Affairs
   D the Department of Justice

5. What piece of legislation broke up most Indian reservations?
   A the Morrill Act
   B the Thirteenth Amendment
   C the Homestead Act
   D the Dawes Act

6. The Comstock Lode was an example of what western phenomenon during the 1800s?
   A fighting Indians wars
   B discovering precious metals in the ground
   C traveling west to Oregon and California
   D taking cattle on long cattle drives

7. Panning for gold was an example of what kind of mining?
   A hydraulic mining
   B placer mining
   C hard-rock mining
   D strip mining

8. What was the purpose of the Chisholm Trail?
   A to allow Native Americans to travel from one reservation to another
   B to allow settlers to travel to Oregon
   C to allow cowboys to take large numbers of cattle to rail centers
   D to transport gold and silver back East

9. Which invention encouraged the spread of privately owned cattle ranches?
   A the Texas longhorn
   B barbed wire
   C the Comstock Lode
   D placer mining

10. What advantage did railroad companies have in building westward?
    A They could use slave labor.
    B They were given permission to build wherever they wanted.
    C They could use buffalo as a natural resource.
    D The government provided them with land.

11. Which of the following settlers were known as Exodusters?
    A white settlers
    B Chinese settlers
    C African American settlers
    D European settlers

12. Why did many western settlers build dugouts and sod houses?
    A Their building supplies had been lost on the journey.
    B They preferred them to wood-framed houses.
    C Lumber was often scarce.
    D They kept out insects.

13. Which of the following was a hardship faced by western farmers?
    A lack of wind
    B lack of water
    C industrial pollution
    D lack of land

14. What were the terms of the Homestead Act?
    A Any head of a household could claim 160 acres if he or she farmed the land for five years.
    B Any head of a household could move into a government-built home for free.
    C Any head of a household could purchase a house from the government at a reduced rate.
    D Any head of a household could receive a free train ticket west.

15. What was the name for large farms that were operated like factories?
    A bonanza farms
    B dugouts
    C sod houses
    D factory farms

16. Read the following quote by the historian Frederick Jackson Turner and answer the question below.

> Up to our own day American history has been in a large degree the history of the colonization of the Great West. The existence of an area of free land, its continuous recession [moving back], and the advance of American settlement westward, explain American development.

Which of the following represents a modern historian's criticism of Turner's idea?
    A America's westward expansion was an important part of American identity.
    B The term *frontier* should not apply to an area that was already inhabited by Native Americans.
    C Most Americans were not interested in the frontier.
    D Americans never believed in manifest destiny.

17. How were sod houses built?
    A by building a frame and planting grass and shrubs on it
    B by digging out a shelter from the side of a hill
    C by cutting blocks of turf and soil out of the prairie and stacking them
    D by constructing a house out of wood and insulating it with sod

18. **Expository Writing** Write a brief explanation of how the government provided opportunities and protection for western settlers.

The Second Industrial Revolution

Test Preparation

DIRECTIONS Read each question and circle the letter of the best response.

1. The Bessemer process affected which of the following materials?
   A oil
   B steel
   C steam
   D iron

2. What was another name for oil prospectors who dug wells looking for oil?
   A wildcatters
   B linesmen
   C wellheads
   D robber barons

3. Why was Spindletop Hill in Texas an important location?
   A It was home to many large steel mills.
   B It was the largest train depot in Texas.
   C It was home to former slaves.
   D It was the center of Texas's oil boom.

4. The transcontinental railroad connected the East to the West in what year?
   A 1829
   B 1849
   C 1869
   D 1889

5. Rural dwellers benefited from which of the following developments in mass marketing?
   A advertising focused on women
   B department stores
   C mail-order companies
   D clever brand names

6. Which of the following was a side effect of the railroad industry?
   A time zones
   B electricity
   C labor unions
   D oil trusts

7. What is the name for an economic system in which private businesses run most industries?
   A monopoly
   B laissez-faire
   C capitalism
   D corporation

8. Which philosophy emphasized that inequalities were part of a natural order?
   A social Darwinism
   B laissez-faire
   C capitalism
   D trusts

9. Which of the following best describes vertical integration?
   A acquiring companies that compete with you
   B selling shares of your business as stocks
   C gaining complete control over an industry
   D acquiring companies that supply your business

10. What did critics call men like Andrew Carnegie and Cornelius Vanderbilt?
    A entrepreneurs
    B robber barons
    C captains of industry
    D tycoons

11. Which industry did Andrew Carnegie control?
    A steel
    B oil
    C railroads
    D electricity

12. What was the goal of the Sherman Antitrust Act?
    A to allow corporations to form monopolies
    B to limit the power of corporations
    C to provide fair wages to employees
    D to establish sweatshops

13. How long did most unskilled laborers work?
    A 10 hours a day, six days a week
    B 10 hours a day, seven days a week
    C 12 hours a day, six days a week
    D 12 hours a day, seven days a week

14. What was the purpose of the Knights of Labor?
    A to create a monopoly in the oil industry
    B to fight for better pay and safer conditions for workers
    C to lobby the government for enforcement of the Sherman Antitrust Act
    D to make sure workers did not strike or close down factories

15. Xenophobia resulted from which of the following?
    A the Haymarket Riot
    B the Great Railroad Strike
    C the Homestead Strike
    D the Pullman Strike

16. Which of the following was something employers used to hurt labor unions?
    A monopolies
    B blacklists
    C sweatshops
    D xenophobia

17. What city was home to the nation's first subway system?
    A Philadelphia
    B San Francisco
    C New York City
    D Boston

18. Who is known as the inventor of the telephone?
    A Elisha Gray
    B Alexander Graham Bell
    C Samuel F. B. Morse
    D Thomas Edison

19. In what year did Orville and Wilbur Wright successfully test their airplane at Kitty Hawk, North Carolina?
    A 1883
    B 1893
    C 1903
    D 1913

20. How did Thomas Edison draw attention to his invention of the light bulb?
    A He advertised it in catalogs.
    B He sold it door-to-door.
    C He brought electricity to parts of New York City.
    D He held countless demonstrations.

21. **Descriptive Writing** Write a short journal entry describing your experience traveling to Wall Street from your small farm outside of New York City in the year 1882. Be sure to include details of city life.

Life at the Turn of the 20th Century   Test Preparation

DIRECTIONS Read each question and circle the letter of the best response.

1. During the late 1800s, most immigrants came from what part of Europe?
   A northern and western Europe
   B Scandinavia
   C eastern and southern Europe
   D the British Isles

2. Over the course of 62 years, approximately 12 million Europeans passed through which immigration station in New York Harbor?
   A Angel Island
   B Ellis Island
   C Statue of Liberty
   D Alcatraz

3. Why were there so many ethnic neighborhoods in large cities?
   A The government forced immigrants to live in ethnic groups.
   B Immigrants liked to live near other people from their homeland.
   C Each factory only hired members of one ethnic group.
   D Ethnic groups could only find housing suitable for them in certain areas.

4. Who could immigrants turn to for help?
   A the factory manager
   B the local mayor
   C benevolent societies
   D the police department

5. What was another name for Americans who opposed immigration?
   A nativists
   B tenements
   C reformers
   D emigrants

6. The Chinese Exclusion Act included which of the following?
   A a boycott of Chinese goods for 10 years
   B the removal of all Chinese immigrants from California
   C the imprisonment of all Chinese immigrants
   D an end to Chinese immigration for 10 years

7. Which of the following was a method that nativists tried to use to keep immigrants out of the United States?
   A literacy tests
   B benevolent societies
   C poll taxes
   D union organizing

8. What new invention made taller buildings more practical for inhabitants?
   A immigrant labor
   B elevators
   C urban planning
   D steel frames

9. Which of the following was Frederick Law Olmsted's most famous work?
   A the Social Gospel
   B Ellis Island
   C the Chinese Exclusion Act
   D Central Park in New York City

10. Which of the following best describes tenements?
    A middle-class neighborhoods full of single-family homes
    B rundown apartment buildings that were overcrowded and unhealthy
    C carefully planned city parks made to look like the countryside
    D volunteer centers where the poor could receive assistance

11. Where could the poor find assistance from social reformers?
    A immigration centers
    B tenements
    C skyscrapers
    D settlement houses

12. What was a negative aspect of political machines?
    A They were usually corrupt.
    B They did not help immigrants.
    C They were unable to control cities.
    D They often lost elections.

13. Which of the following characterizes the federal government in the late 1800s?
    A Government officials worked hard to improve the lives of the poor.
    B Government officials were often involved in profitable scandals.
    C Government officials were quiet, dutiful servants to their voters.
    D Government officials were constantly thrown in jail on corruption charges.

14. Which of the following was a major problem for farmers in the late 1800s?
    A Prices for farm equipment dropped.
    B Inflation drove up crop prices.
    C Oversupply of crops drove prices down, which hurt farmers' income.
    D The largest farmers often had to pay the highest shipping prices.

15. Which group lobbied state governments to regulate the railroads?
    A political machines
    B the National Grange
    C the Grant administration
    D immigrants

16. Why did the Supreme Court agree that the government had the right to regulate railroad companies?
    A because railroad companies were privately owned
    B because not many people were affected by railroad rates
    C because railroads had a long history of corruption
    D because railroad rates involved the public interest

17. Which political party fought for the causes of farmers and the working class?
    A the Populist Party
    B the Democratic Party
    C the Republican Party
    D the Reformer Party

18. Who made up most of the victims of lynching?
    A farmers
    B African Americans
    C social reformers
    D bankers

19. Which of the following had the effect of legalizing segregation for nearly 60 years?
    A poll taxes
    B the Niagara Movement
    C the gold standard
    D *Plessy* v. *Ferguson*

20. **Descriptive Writing** Write an essay comparing the daily lives of immigrants, farmers, and African Americans in the late 1800s. Be sure to include details about each group and their experiences.

The Progressives

DIRECTIONS Read each question and circle the letter of the best response.

1. Which of the following best describes the movement known as progressivism?
   A the attempt to improve the lives of the working class and to regulate the unchecked power of business
   B the attempt to limit the size of government
   C the attempt to encourage business growth and to build a strong middle class
   D the attempt to safeguard the upper class from crime and labor unrest

2. What were journalists working for reform called?
   A organizers
   B strike breakers
   C muckrakers
   D scalawags

3. The Triangle Shirtwaist Company Fire brought attention to what national problem?
   A forest fires
   B unsafe working conditions
   C high-priced clothing
   D racial tensions

4. Why did many American cities adopt the commission plan of city government?
   A It was more honest and efficient than previous forms of government.
   B It was an effective political machine.
   C It allowed voters to directly influence public policy.
   D It maintained total control.

5. Which of the following gave Americans more control over their government?
   A New Freedom
   B the Elkins Act
   C the Seventeenth Amendment
   D the Hepburn Act

6. What was the name for a proposal placed on the ballot by voters?
   A referendum
   B initiative
   C union
   D recall

7. Which of the following refers to the proposed ban on making, selling, and distributing alcoholic beverages?
   A referendum
   B suffrage
   C prohibition
   D preservation

8. Why were suffragists upset over the passage of the Fifteenth Amendment?
   A It allowed African American men to vote but not women.
   B It specifically stated that women could not vote.
   C It gave civil rights to men but not to women.
   D It ended slavery for men but not for women.

9. What was the name of Theodore Roosevelt's policy of balancing the needs of workers, business, and consumers?
   A progressivism
   B the Square Deal
   C prohibition
   D New Freedom

The Progressives   Test Preparation

10. What was Theodore Roosevelt's policy toward monopolies and trusts?
    A If they were showing large profits, he tried to break them up.
    B He approved of all monopolies and trusts that did not break any laws.
    C If they were acting against the public interest, he tried to break them up.
    D He disapproved of all monopolies and trusts.

11. Upton Sinclair's novel *The Jungle* helped lead to which of the following?
    A the Meat Inspection Act
    B the Hepburn Act
    C the Newlands Reclamation Act
    D the Elkins Act

12. How were Theodore Roosevelt's views on the environment different from those of previous presidents?
    A He thought there should be more logging in the West.
    B He realized that natural resources were limited.
    C He thought that there was enough coal available for another industrial revolution.
    D He wanted to preserve most of the American West in its natural state.

13. Which of the following issues caused a split among suffragists?
    A whether to use a state-by-state approach or a federal approach
    B whether or not to support the war effort
    C whether or not to support abolition
    D whether or not voting would interfere with women's duties at home

14. What was Woodrow Wilson's reputation as a politician?
    A a zealous reformer
    B a strong supporter of business
    C a suffragist
    D the leader of a political machine

15. What was the goal of the Clayton Antitrust Act?
    A to give more freedom to corporations
    B to limit the power of labor unions
    C to make it more difficult for businesses to form monopolies
    D to discontinue the Sherman Antitrust Act

16. Which amendment gave women the right to vote?
    A the Seventeenth Amendment
    B the Eighteenth Amendment
    C the Nineteenth Amendment
    D the Twentieth Amendment

17. The Federal Reserve Act focused on which of the following Progressive goals?
    A tariff reductions
    B banking reform
    C stronger antitrust legislation
    D environmental protection

18. **Persuasive Writing** Write a letter to a friend arguing either for or against the Progressive cause. Include details about specific issues, including business regulations, workplace conditions, and women's rights.

Entering the World Stage

Test Preparation

DIRECTIONS Read each question and circle the letter of the best response.

1. Which of the following ideologies contributed to imperialism?
   A racial tolerance
   B cultural superiority
   C women's rights
   D belief in equality

2. Which of the following groups influenced Hawaiian politics?
   A shipbuilders
   B industrialists
   C sugarcane plantation owners
   D Japanese businessmen

3. Who possessed spheres of influence in China?
   A American businesses
   B European nations
   C the steel industry
   D various Chinese ethnic groups

4. Why did the U.S. government propose the Open Door Policy?
   A It sought to build naval bases in China.
   B It wanted to allow immigration from China.
   C It wanted to modernize China.
   D It lacked a sphere of influence in China.

5. What was a result of the Boxer Rebellion?
   A Support for the Open Door Policy increased.
   B China became closed to outsiders.
   C The rebellion took over the Chinese government.
   D The Chinese population decided it liked having contact with European powers.

6. Which of the following was a result of the Russo-Japanese War?
   A Japan conquered Russia.
   B Japan became the strongest power in East Asia.
   C Japan was defeated by Russia.
   D Japan remained in a weakened state for decades.

7. Which of the following helped lead to the Spanish-American War?
   A the Boxer Rebellion
   B dollar diplomacy
   C the Tampico incident
   D yellow journalism

8. Who did the de Lôme letter ridicule as being "weak and catering to the rabble"?
   A William McKinley
   B George Dewey
   C William Randolph Hearst
   D Theodore Roosevelt

9. What was the name of the regiment organized by Theodore Roosevelt to fight in Cuba?
   A the San Juan Regiment
   B the Rough Riders
   C the Imperialists
   D the Adventurers

10. What happened in the Philippines after the United States annexed it as a territory?
   A Filipinos welcomed the Americans as liberators.
   B Filipinos formed an alliance with Spain.
   C The U.S. Army fought Filipino rebels for three years.
   D The U.S. Army reconstructed Manila and held elections.

Entering the World Stage   Test Preparation

11. Which of the following best describes Cuba's relationship with the United States after 1901?
    A Cuba was a protectorate.
    B Cuba was a U.S. territory.
    C Cuba was a U.S. state.
    D Cuba was still part of Spain.

12. Why did Theodore Roosevelt support Panamanian revolutionaries in their fight against Colombia?
    A The United States was at war with Colombia.
    B He cared about the well-being of Panamanians.
    C He wanted to build a canal through the Isthmus of Panama.
    D The United States was at war with Spain.

13. Which policy promoted American economic interests in other countries and used that economic power to achieve American policy goals?
    A imperialism
    B dollar diplomacy
    C the Roosevelt Corollary
    D spheres of influence

14. What was the Roosevelt Corollary?
    A It declared the Western Hemisphere off-limits to further colonization by European powers.
    B It declared that the United States would punish any European nation that traded with Latin America.
    C It threatened to attack any Latin American nation that attacked a European nation.
    D It stated that the United States reserved the right to intervene in the internal affairs of Latin American countries.

15. Which Mexican dictator ruled from 1877 to 1910?
    A Francisco Madero
    B Victoriano Huerta
    C Porfirio Díaz
    D Emiliano Zapata

16. Why did President Woodrow Wilson order a military expedition to hunt down Francisco "Pancho" Villa?
    A He was responsible for the Tampico incident.
    B He was an oppressive dictator.
    C He opposed the U.S.-supported candidate for president.
    D He led an attack on an American town.

17. Why did American leaders fear the leadership of Emiliano Zapata?
    A He might attack the United States.
    B U.S. economic interests might be harmed by the redistribution of land that Zapata wanted.
    C He might become an oppressive leader.
    D He might industrialize Mexico and create competition for American industries.

18. Mediation by Argentina, Brazil, and Chile avoided crisis after which of the following conflicts?
    A the Tampico incident
    B the Battle of Veracruz
    C the Battle of San Juan Hill
    D the Mexican Revolution

19. **Expository Writing** Write a brief newspaper article explaining how the United States got involved in the Spanish-American War.

The First World War

Test Preparation

DIRECTIONS Read each question and circle the letter of the best response.

1. The European practice of militarism included which of the following?
   A nations constantly attacking their neighbors
   B nations building up militaries in order to be prepared for war
   C nations acquiring colonies overseas
   D nations agreeing to maintain small armies

2. Which of the following was a benefit of colonial empires?
   A They protected countries from attack.
   B They created a balance of power.
   C They provided a large work force.
   D They provided markets and natural resources.

3. Which army made the first attack in World War I?
   A the Russian army
   B the German army
   C the British army
   D the French army

4. Which nations made up the Central Powers?
   A Austria-Hungary, Germany, and the Ottoman Empire
   B Great Britain, France, and Russia
   C Belgium, France, and Germany
   D Austria-Hungary, Russia, and Great Britain

5. Which of the following was considered by some military officials to be unfair and barbaric?
   A trench warfare
   B machine guns
   C tanks
   D poisonous gas

6. Use the table below to answer the following question.

Somme Statistics
Duration of battle: July 1—Nov. 18, 1916
Total Allied casualties: about 630,000
British casualties on day 1: about 57,000
Total German casualties: about 650,000

Which of the following might have contributed to the high number of casualties of the Battle of the Somme?
   A the weather conditions
   B the length of the battle
   C the local population
   D the use of field rifles

7. Which of the following best describes isolationism?
   A seeking influence over foreign nations
   B wishing to expand territorially
   C wanting to avoid involvement in the affairs of other nations
   D attempting to isolate one's enemies

8. Which of the following proposed an alliance between Germany and Mexico?
   A the Zimmerman Note
   B the *Sussex* pledge
   C the Schlieffen Plan
   D the Selective Service Act

The First World War   Test Preparation

9. What event pushed the U.S. government into declaring war on Germany in March 1917?
   A the German use of poisonous gas on Allied troops
   B the German sinking of three American merchant ships
   C the Zimmerman Note
   D the *Sussex* pledge

10. How did the U.S. government build an army in a short amount of time?
   A by asking for volunteers
   B by appealing to the patriotism of Americans
   C by establishing the draft
   D by offering large signing bonuses

11. The War Industries Board had the authority to do which of the following?
   A regulate all materials needed in the war effort
   B manage and increase food production
   C set production goals and prices for fuels
   D collect Liberty bonds from American citizens

12. Besides negotiating disputes between workers and management during the war, what did the National War Labor Board accomplish?
   A It took over the operation of all factories and their labor forces.
   B It established a draft system for the army and navy.
   C It outlawed all labor unions.
   D It established the eight-hour workday and promoted equal pay for women.

13. What is another name for the right of people to decide their own political status?
   A imperialism
   B self-determination
   C reparations
   D militarism

14. How did Woodrow Wilson hope to ensure world peace?
   A by establishing the League of Nations
   B by giving the Big Four control over all world affairs
   C by eliminating every nation's military
   D by making Germany admit it was guilty of starting World War I

15. Which of the following best describes reparations?
   A the former colonies of Germany that were given to the Allies
   B various components of Wilson's Fourteen Points
   C the policies of the League of Nations
   D billions of dollars that Germany had to pay to the Allies

16. Which document officially ended World War I?
   A the Treaty of Ghent
   B the Treaty of Versailles
   C the Fourteen Points
   D the Treaty of Paris

17. **Narrative Writing** Describe the daily life of a World War I soldier. Include details of warfare.

From War to Peace   Test Preparation

DIRECTIONS Read each question and circle the letter of the best response.

1. Who were the Bolsheviks?
   A revolutionaries who attempted to undermine capitalism in America
   B a group of German immigrants who wanted to establish a new social system
   C a group led by Vladimir I. Lenin who took charge of Russia after the revolution
   D Americans who led an attack on suspected radicals

2. What is the name for a social system with no economic classes and no private property?
   A capitalism
   B communism
   C radicalism
   D conservatism

3. The Palmer raids were a direct result of what national phenomenon?
   A labor unrest
   B the assembly line
   C the Red Scare
   D prohibition

4. Who wrote, "There can be no right to strike against the public safety by anybody, anywhere, anytime"?
   A Samuel Gompers
   B Calvin Coolidge
   C Woodrow Wilson
   D John L. Lewis

5. What is the name for radicals who want to overthrow the government?
   A immigrants
   B labor organizers
   C anarchists
   D nativists

6. What was significant about the trial of Nicola Sacco and Bartolomeo Vanzetti?
   A Their political ideas played a major role in their criminal trial.
   B They were both extremely violent murderers.
   C They had belonged to an influential labor union.
   D They were both found innocent.

7. What was the greatest benefit of the assembly line?
   A It allowed every worker to perform multiple tasks.
   B It made the work more interesting.
   C It created higher quality products.
   D It allowed for much higher production speeds.

8. Why did Henry Ford pay his workers more than the average factory wages?
   A The government required him to.
   B He wanted them to buy cars.
   C He wanted to compensate them for their boring, repetitive jobs.
   D The unions demanded it.

9. In which city did Henry Ford base his manufacturing operations?
   A New York
   B Chicago
   C Detroit
   D Buffalo

10. Company-paid pensions are an example of which of the following?
    A productivity
    B welfare capitalism
    C credit
    D reparations

From War to Peace   # Test Preparation

11. By the end of the 1920s, 4 homes in 10 had which of the following?
    A a radio
    B a refrigerator
    C a vacuum cleaner
    D a car

12. What is the name for paying for an item over time in small payments?
    A buying on credit
    B buying on margin
    C installment buying
    D welfare capitalism

13. What natural disaster caused Florida to sink into an economic depression?
    A an infestation of insects
    B a hurricane
    C a flood
    D a drought

14. What was Warren G. Harding's attitude toward the presidency?
    A He saw it as a bully pulpit.
    B He saw it as a chance to fight for national security.
    C He saw it as a chance to regulate business.
    D He saw it as a largely ceremonial position.

15. What was Harding's attitude toward government and business?
    A "Less government in business and more business in government."
    B "What's good for the White House is good for business."
    C "More government in business and less business in government."
    D "What's good for the Federal Trade Commission is good for business."

16. What crime was committed in the Teapot Dome scandal?
    A Government officials regulated oil companies.
    B Government officials accepted bribes from oil companies.
    C Oil companies stole money from the government.
    D Representatives of oil companies received government posts.

17. Calvin Coolidge's presidency was characterized by his unshakable faith in which of the following?
    A business
    B the government
    C labor unions
    D churches

18. What was the goal of the Kellogg-Briand Pact?
    A to prevent war
    B to limit military buildup
    C to force European nations to repay their war debts
    D to end the use of tariffs

19. What is the name for a competition between nations to build more and more weapons?
    A reparations
    B imperialism
    C arms race
    D capitalism

20. **Expository Writing** Write a brief essay describing how Americans had very different experiences during the 1920s. Include consumers, farmers, and immigrants.

The Roaring Twenties

Test Preparation

DIRECTIONS Read each question and circle the letter of the best response.

1. What was the name given to women who defied traditional ideas of proper dress and behavior?
   A radicals
   B flappers
   C fundamentalists
   D evolutionists

2. Which of the following was true of female voters in the 1920s?
   A They supported sweeping changes in the national government.
   B They voted for more social programs.
   C They tended to vote much as their husbands, fathers, or other men in their lives voted.
   D They represented a distinctive group of voters.

3. What was one effect of hard times for farmers?
   A Many city dwellers bought farms at a low price.
   B Many people from farming communities moved to cities.
   C Stores began importing food from overseas.
   D Food became so expensive that city dwellers went hungry.

4. Why did the Ku Klux Klan grow dramatically in the 1920s?
   A It no longer used violent tactics.
   B It started accepting Jewish and Catholic members.
   C It encouraged the shift in values in urban America.
   D New members thought it could help them preserve their place in society.

5. Why did fundamentalists oppose the teaching of evolution?
   A They believed it went against the biblical account of how God created humans.
   B They supported a more scientific approach.
   C They thought it violated freedom of speech.
   D They believed in a symbolic interpretation of the Bible.

6. Which of the following caused problems for federal authorities during Prohibition?
   A immigrants and flappers
   B bootleggers and speakeasies
   C members of the Ku Klux Klan and settlement houses
   D the Harlem Renaissance and bootleggers

7. What lured many African Americans to northern cities during World War I?
   A an abundance of factory jobs
   B new urban culture
   C racial tolerance
   D Christian fundamentalism

8. What was the name for this movement of African Americans northward?
   A the Harlem Renaissance
   B the Ku Klux Klan
   C the Great Migration
   D Christian fundamentalism

9. What was the name for an artistic and cultural movement among African Americans during the 1920s?
   A jazz
   B the Harlem Renaissance
   C the Great Migration
   D fundamentalism

The Roaring Twenties

Test Preparation

10. Which African American leader promoted self-reliance, economic success, and racial pride?
    A Marcus Garvey
    B W.E.B. Du Bois
    C Langston Hughes
    D Zora Neale Hurston

11. Who was Louis Armstrong?
    A an artist of the Harlem Renaissance
    B an influential poet and writer
    C a legendary jazz musician
    D a choreographer and dancer

12. Why was *The Birth of a Nation* influential?
    A It was the first "talkie," featuring spoken dialogue.
    B It was the first film to feature a cartoon character.
    C It helped establish film as an art form.
    D It captured the drama of Charles Lindbergh's transatlantic flight.

13. How did radio and movies help develop a national culture?
    A They provided Americans with a shared experience.
    B They encouraged the development of new technology.
    C They supported the expansion of education.
    D They advertised the latest artwork and literature.

14. Who achieved "the greatest feat of a solitary man in the history of the human race"?
    A Charles A. Lindbergh
    B F. Scott Fitzgerald
    C William Jennings Bryan
    D Charlie Chaplin

15. Which of the following writers was concerned with leading social issues of the day?
    A Willa Cather
    B Gertrude Stein
    C Edith Wharton
    D Edna St. Vincent Millay

16. What was George Gershwin's contribution to popular culture in the 1920s?
    A composing music
    B acting in movies
    C playing baseball
    D writing novels

17. *The Great Gatsby* was written by which great American novelist?
    A Ernest Hemingway
    B Sinclair Lewis
    C F. Scott Fitzgerald
    D Gertrude Stein

18. The Lost Generation included which of the following?
    A farmers who did not participate in the economic growth of the 1920s
    B American writers who lived in Europe after World War I
    C Christians who did not support fundamentalism
    D sports heroes who led troubled lives

19. **Persuasive Writing** Write a persuasive essay arguing that you would have enjoyed living in the 1920s more than any other decade you have studied so far. Compare the 1920s to previous decades and include examples of lifestyle and culture that appeal to you.

The Great Depression Begins

Test Preparation

DIRECTIONS Read each question and circle the letter of the best response.

1. What is the name for the total value of goods and services produced in a nation during a specific period?
   A wealth distribution
   B stock value
   C gross national product
   D foreclosures

2. Why did union membership drop during the 1920s?
   A Employers expanded welfare capitalism programs.
   B High unemployment rates limited the political power of labor unions.
   C Workers who did not participate in unions were offered shorter work hours and bigger paychecks.
   D The government took over many of the responsibilities of labor unions.

3. What was one reason Herbert Hoover won the presidency in 1928?
   A He was a natural politician.
   B He opposed Prohibition.
   C He supported the interests of business.
   D He drew support from Catholic urban immigrant populations.

4. What happened to the personal savings rate during the 1920s?
   A It increased noticeably.
   B It increased somewhat.
   C It decreased somewhat.
   D It decreased noticeably.

5. Analyze this graph in order to answer the question below.

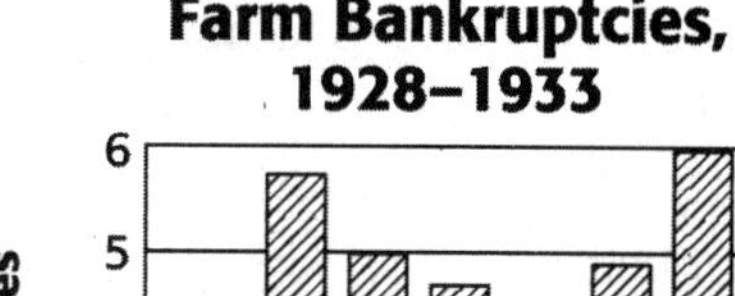

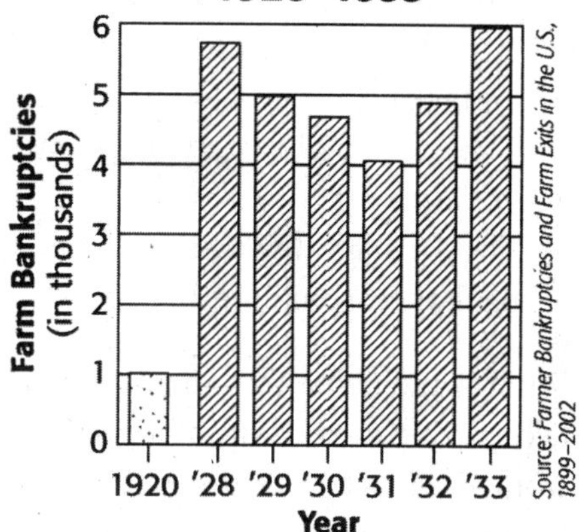

In what year did approximately 5,000 farms go bankrupt?
   A 1928
   B 1929
   C 1930
   D 1931

6. Black Tuesday included which of the following?
   A a race to take advantage of low stock prices
   B Herbert Hoover's intervention in the stock market
   C an effort by leading bankers to prevent a further collapse in stock prices
   D a huge drop in the value of the stock market

7. What was the practice of purchasing stocks with loans from stockbrokers called?
   A security buying
   B buying on credit
   C buying on margin
   D foreclosing

The Great Depression Begins Test Preparation

8. How were businesses affected by the stock market crash?
   A They were forced to hire more workers.
   B They lost large amounts of money on the stock market.
   C They received large loans from the government.
   D They lost money as customers cut back their spending.

9. What is the name for a bank or lender taking over ownership of a property from an owner who has failed to make loan payments?
   A foreclosure
   B bank run
   C bankruptcy
   D margin call

10. How did European nations respond to the crisis?
   A by passing high tariffs
   B by loaning money to the U.S. government
   C by hiring American workers
   D by exporting more products

11. What was a Hooverville?
   A another name for the White House
   B a shantytown full of homeless people
   C a farm that suffered foreclosure
   D a town that was given assistance by the federal government

12. Which of the following was one of the human causes of the Dust Bowl?
   A careless agricultural practices
   B the use of tractors
   C the drought
   D buying on margin

13. What was the name given to people that left the Great Plains during the 1930s?
   A refugees
   B Okies
   C hoboes
   D Hoovers

14. What did Woody Guthrie do during the 1930s?
   A He established a system of charities to help the unemployed.
   B He lobbied the government for assistance to farmers.
   C He wrote songs about the hardships caused by the Dust Bowl.
   D He opened new banks.

15. The construction of the Hoover Dam exemplified which of the following?
   A the associative state
   B "rugged individualism"
   C a cooperative
   D the Dust Bowl

16. **Expository Writing** Write an essay describing the causes and effects of the Great Depression. Include at least two causes and two effects. Be sure to write an introduction and conclusion.

The New Deal   Test Preparation

---

1. Public works programs would provide which of the following?
   A food
   B shelter
   C relief payments
   D jobs

2. What kind of politician was Franklin Delano Roosevelt?
   A a reform-minded Democrat
   B a traditional Democrat
   C a reform-minded Republican
   D a traditional Republican

3. How did Roosevelt's fireside chats win him the lasting support of voters?
   A by clarifying his positions on various political issues
   B by allowing the public to meet him in person
   C by establishing a personal connection with the public
   D by providing a humorous outlook in the face of hardship

4. How did the Second New Deal differ from Roosevelt's earlier programs?
   A It ended most direct payments to Americans in need and focused on work relief.
   B It attempted to decrease the federal budget deficit.
   C It focused on reforms that would help prevent serious economic crises in the future.
   D It sought relief for those hit hardest by the Great Depression.

5. As soon as Roosevelt took office, what crisis did he deal with?
   A widespread unemployment
   B the hunger problem
   C the troubled banking industry
   D the unstable stock market

6. What were the three goals of the New Deal?
   A reorganization, renewal, and recovery
   B education, caution, and investigation
   C relief, recovery, and reforms
   D reforms, reparations, and religion

7. What was the purpose of the Civilian Conservation Corps?
   A to raise money for the government
   B to employ young men
   C to encourage good citizenship
   D to transform soldiers into farmers

8. Which program provided income to older Americans and unemployment insurance to those that lost their jobs?
   A Social Security
   B Works Progress Administration
   C agricultural subsidies
   D Civilian Conservation Corps

9. Which law enacted a minimum wage?
   A the Fair Labor Standards Act
   B the National Labor Relations Act
   C the National Industrial Recovery Act
   D the Social Security Act

The New Deal   Test Preparation

---

10. How did Roosevelt try to help labor unions?
    A by creating company-sponsored unions
    B by starting government factories that employed union labor
    C by negotiating better contracts for them
    D by protecting the right of workers to organize

11. What was one accomplishment of the Rural Electrification Act?
    A providing electricity to the elderly
    B increasing the number of rural houses with electricity
    C giving power generators to farmers
    D requiring power companies to serve remote areas

12. Why did some critics oppose Roosevelt's plan to add more justices to the Supreme Court?
    A They believed it would interfere with New Deal programs.
    B They thought it would help him win the election.
    C They thought it would upset the constitutional balance of power.
    D They feared that an expanded Supreme Court would support the interests of business.

13. What was notable about Frances Perkins?
    A She was the first woman to head an executive department.
    B She gave Roosevelt the idea for Social Security.
    C She photographed the rural poor throughout the 1930s.
    D She led the Black Cabinet and worked for civil rights.

14. Why were movies so popular during the 1930s?
    A They supplied news about the latest New Deal programs.
    B They provided a dignified record of the lives of the rural poor.
    C They brought religion, music, and sports to Americans.
    D They helped Americans to escape from their problems.

15. Which of the following made important reforms to banks and the stock market?
    A the Tennessee Valley Authority and the Security and Exchange Commission
    B the Federal Deposit Insurance Corporation and the Securities and Exchange Commission
    C the Federal Deposit Insurance Corporation and the Social Security Act
    D the Works Progress Administration and the Rural Electrification Act

16. **Expository Writing** Picture life in a large town in the Midwest during the Great Depression. Write a description of how the New Deal affected life in the town. Include details about specific New Deal programs.

World War II Erupts
Test Preparation

DIRECTIONS Read each question and circle the letter of the best response.

1. How did the Treaty of Versailles affect Germany?
   A Germany was weakened and suffered frequent attacks from its neighbors.
   B The economy was damaged and suffered from inflation.
   C Germany's economy rebounded.
   D Communists took control of Germany.

2. Which of the following best characterizes fascism?
   A a system of government that glorifies the state
   B a system of government that distributes wealth equally
   C a system of government that empowers large corporations
   D a system of government that tries to stay out of business and personal affairs

3. How did Adolph Hitler build support?
   A by blaming Communists and Socialists for Germany's economic problems
   B by advocating extensive reforms to the German government
   C by spreading the myth of Aryan greatness and the coming German empire
   D by leading a military coup

4. As soon as Hitler gained power in Germany, he began to do which of the following?
   A build up the German military
   B pursue economic reforms
   C establish public works programs
   D seek an alliance with Italy

5. Which of the following was one of Hitler's most useful skills?
   A economic analysis
   B public speaking
   C military strategy
   D diplomatic relations

6. Besides Italy, which nations became involved in military conflict in the mid-1930s?
   A Japan, Germany, and Spain
   B Switzerland, France, and Spain
   C Japan, Germany, and Great Britain
   D Sweden, Great Britain, and Japan

7. What nation did Italy invade in 1935?
   A Great Britain
   B France
   C Ethiopia
   D Greece

8. What characteristic did Italy share with Germany in the 1930s?
   A a destroyed economy
   B high inflation
   C a Fascist government
   D postwar humiliation

9. Great Britain and France declared war after Germany invaded which country?
   A Austria
   B Czechoslovakia
   C Poland
   D Belgium

10. Why did Stalin agree to a nonaggression pact with Hitler?
   A Stalin feared the growing power of Britain and France.
   B Stalin supported Hitler's intentions.
   C Stalin wanted to invade Poland without going to war with Germany.
   D Stalin believed the deal offered the greatest possible security.

Test Preparation

World War II Erupts   # Test Preparation

11. The most significant scientific program of World War II involved the creation of which of the following?
    A a faster fighter plane
    B synthetic rubber
    C an atomic bomb
    D the U-boat

12. Who made up the Axis Powers?
    A Germany, Italy, and Japan
    B Germany, Norway, and France
    C France, Great Britain, and Spain
    D Great Britain, Italy, and the United States

13. What is the name for the policy of giving in to aggressive demands in order to maintain peace?
    A isolationism
    B appeasement
    C pacifism
    D neutrality

14. The Atlantic Charter proclaimed the shared goals of which two nations?
    A Germany and the Soviet Union
    B the United States and France
    C the United States and Britain
    D Italy and Japan

15. Which event led the United States to enter World War II?
    A Japan's attack on Pearl Harbor
    B Germany's U-boat attack in the Atlantic Ocean
    C Germany's attack on London
    D Italy's attack in North Africa

16. What did Rosie the Riveter symbolize?
    A the growing aircraft industry
    B women in the workplace
    C the use of new technology
    D women in science

17. Which of the following best describes the Battle of Britain?
    A a battle between infantry and artillery
    B a battle between air forces
    C a battle between navies
    D a battle between U-boats and merchant ships

18. Which of the following represents one reason American forces at Pearl Harbor were unable to defend the base?
    A No single commander was in charge of Pearl Harbor's defenses.
    B The Japanese possessed more advanced technology than the Americans.
    C Americans were ordered not to fire a single shot.
    D Routine defensive steps malfunctioned on the day of the attack.

19. Which program brought Mexicans across the border temporarily to work in the United States?
    A the Manhattan Project
    B the Zoot Suit Program
    C the Bracero Program
    D the War Production Program

20. **Expository Writing** Describe the various ways the U.S. government prepared the nation for World War II.

The United States in World War II

Test Preparation

DIRECTIONS Read each question and circle the letter of the best response.

1. Which of the following threatened the delivery of U.S. supplies to the Allies?
   A code talkers
   B Operation Torch
   C wolf packs
   D kamikaze attacks

2. Which battle marked the beginning of the end for the German invasion of the Soviet Union?
   A the Battle of Stalingrad
   B the Battle of El Alamein
   C the Battle of Leningrad
   D the Battle of Anzio

3. Why was it important for the Allies to control North Africa?
   A North Africa had many vital resources.
   B Germany had many troops stationed there.
   C They needed to secure oil coming from the Middle East.
   D Losing it would have been a moral defeat.

4. After succeeding in North Africa, what was the Allies' next target?
   A Italy
   B Germany
   C the Soviet Union
   D France

5. What date did D-Day represent?
   A the German deadline for defeating the Soviet Union
   B the beginning of the Allied attack on mainland Europe
   C the German deadline for invading Great Britain
   D the end of the Allied attack on the German coast

6. The Allied offensive in Western Europe was temporarily set back by which battle?
   A the Battle of the Bulge
   B the Battle of Stalingrad
   C the Battle of Anzio
   D the Battle of Britain

7. Which of the following best describes anti-Semitism?
   A hostility toward or prejudice against Christians
   B feelings of racial superiority
   C hostility toward or prejudice against Jews
   D a tolerance for all religions

8. In addition to the Jews, the Nazi death machine specifically targeted which of the following groups?
   A Communists
   B disabled people
   C women
   D Russians

9. The Final Solution involved which of the following?
   A the establishment of extermination camps for the widespread murder of Jews
   B the Allied invasion of Western Europe
   C the use of atomic bombs to end the war in the Pacific
   D the Allied plan to evacuate all Jews from Europe

10. How did the United States attempt to help European Jews?
    A by publicizing the atrocities committed by the Nazis
    B by bombing concentration camps
    C by forming the War Refugee Board
    D by evacuating Jews from threatened countries

The United States in World War II   Test Preparation

11. Read this table and answer the question below.

Jewish Population Before and After the Holocaust		
	c. 1933	**c. 1950**
Austria	250,000	18,000
Bulgaria	50,000	6,500
Germany	565,000	37,000
Greece	100,000	7,000
Hungary	445,000	155,000
Poland	3,000,000	45,000
Romania	980,000	28,000
Yugoslavia	70,000	3,500

Which country lost the greatest number of Jews during the Holocaust?
A Romania
B Poland
C Germany
D Hungary

12. How did the Allied forces fare against Japanese forces early in the war?
A Japan made small advances, but lacked adequate weapons.
B Japan won most early battles.
C Japan suffered losses, despite superior weapons.
D Japan lost most early battles.

13. Why were the Americans intent on taking Okinawa?
A It had many oil reserves.
B It would be a launching point to attack Japan.
C It held the Japanese headquarters.
D It held ceremonial importance for the Japanese.

14. The Battle of Leyte Gulf saw the first major use of which new Japanese weapon?
A code talkers
B aircraft carriers
C kamikaze attacks
D torpedoes

15. Why were Japanese Americans put in internment camps in the United States during the war?
A The U.S. government feared they would help Japan.
B Americans wanted to seize their property.
C The U.S. government wanted them to teach soldiers how to speak Japanese.
D Americans were afraid they would take over the U.S. government.

16. What was the purpose of the United Nations?
A to prevent the spread of communism and Soviet influence
B to rebuild Japan and Germany as democratic societies
C to encourage cooperation among nations and to prevent future wars
D to punish those who had committed crimes during World War II

17. **Narrative Writing** Summarize the events of World War II, from Germany's invasion of Poland to the American victory over Japan. Include only the most important events of the war.

The Cold War Begins   # Test Preparation

DIRECTIONS Read each question and circle the letter of the best response.

1. What was the Iron Curtain?
   A a defensive military zone
   B a symbolic separation between Soviet and Western powers
   C a region of heavy industry
   D a symbolic separation between industry and agriculture

2. Which U.S. policy involved providing economic aid to other countries in order to strengthen them against the Soviet Union?
   A intervention
   B containment
   C reparations
   D appeasement

3. What was the name for the U.S. effort to help rebuild Europe?
   A the Marshall Plan
   B the Truman Doctrine
   C the Iron Curtain
   D the Berlin Airlift

4. What caused the Berlin Airlift?
   A the Soviet invasion of Eastern Europe
   B an outbreak of influenza in Berlin
   C the Soviets blocking traffic into West Berlin
   D increased international trade

5. Why did Western powers form the North Atlantic Treaty Organization?
   A They feared the size of the Soviet military.
   B They wanted an army capable of invading the Soviet Union.
   C They wanted to promote international trade.
   D They wanted to prevent the spread of communism by providing economic aid to other countries.

6. Which of the following tried to help veterans make a smooth entry into civilian life?
   A the Marshall Plan
   B the GI Bill
   C the Iron Curtain
   D the United Nations

7. How did President Harry S Truman try to expand opportunities for African Americans?
   A by ending segregation in public schools
   B by creating a jobs program for African Americans
   C by prohibiting racial discrimination in the workplace
   D by ending segregation in the military

8. Which of the following was part of Truman's Fair Deal?
   A investment in scientific research
   B a federal health insurance program
   C lower tariffs
   D expansion of the nuclear weapons program

9. Which organization aimed to help poor countries build their economies?
   A the North Atlantic Treaty Organization
   B the United Nations
   C the World Bank
   D the International Monetary Fund

10. Which of the following was called for in the Universal Declaration of Human Rights?
   A equal pay for equal work
   B free elementary education for all people
   C voting rights for all people
   D free housing for all people

The Cold War Begins

Test Preparation

11. Who led the Communist revolution in China?
   A Mao Zedong
   B Syngman Rhee
   C Chiang Kai-shek
   D Kim Il Sung

12. How did Senator Joseph McCarthy earn himself a reputation as the nation's top Communist fighter?
   A by claiming that Communists were working in the U.S. Department of State
   B by prosecuting Ethel and Julius Rosenberg as Communist spies
   C by proving that the U.S. Army was protecting Communists
   D by blacklisting Communist writers and directors in Hollywood

13. McCarthyism included which of the following?
   A prosecuting proven Communists
   B executing radicals who planned to take over the government
   C limiting free speech in order to prevent a Communist takeover
   D spreading fear and making baseless charges

14. What was significant about the 38th parallel?
   A It divided North Korea from South Korea.
   B It separated Japan from South Korea.
   C It was a peaceful border guarded by the United Nations.
   D It was a place of constant warfare after World War II.

15. Why did President Truman think it was important to defend South Korea?
   A It held many strategic resources.
   B It was the best place to stop Communist aggression.
   C It was the best place to station U.S. troops.
   D It held many natural wonders worth protecting.

16. Kim Il Sung led which country?
   A China
   B North Korea
   C South Korea
   D Vietnam

17. The UN forces in Korea began to retreat after which event?
   A the withdrawal of U.S. support
   B a harsh winter
   C an attack from Chinese troops
   D bombardment by Soviet aircraft

18. Which of the following issues created a major obstacle during the peace talks to end the Korean War?
   A whether Korea would be Communist or democratic
   B who would lead the reunited Korea
   C where the boundary between North Korea and China would be
   D where the boundary between North Korea and South Korea would be

19. **Expository Writing** Explain how the Cold War divided major nations between two political spheres. Include examples of specific countries and regions.

Postwar America

Test Preparation

DIRECTIONS Read each question and circle the letter of the best response.

1. What was Dwight D. Eisenhower's main criticism of the Democrats in the 1952 election?
   A their handling of the economy
   B their handling of the Korean War
   C their failure in the Berlin Airlift
   D their policy of brinkmanship

2. Which of the following events brought changes to the Soviet Union in 1953?
   A the launch of *Sputnik*
   B the death of Joseph Stalin
   C the failure of the planned economy
   D the election of President Eisenhower

3. The Warsaw Pact was roughly similar in purpose to which of the following?
   A SEATO
   B the CIA
   C NATO
   D the Eisenhower Doctrine

4. In 1956 the Soviet Union put down rebellions in which two Eastern European nations?
   A Poland and Yugoslavia
   B Hungary and Poland
   C Bulgaria and Romania
   D Romania and Hungary

5. Cold War powers almost went to war over which Middle East location?
   A Iraq
   B the Suez Canal
   C Israel
   D Lebanon

6. Why was the Southeast Asia Treaty Organization formed?
   A to prevent the spread of communism
   B to promote international trade
   C to take control of Vietnam
   D to create a military alliance

7. Which organization was formed in 1947 to collect information about foreign governments?
   A the Central Intelligence Agency
   B the Warsaw Pact
   C the Federal Bureau of Investigation
   D the Federal Civil Defense Administration

8. The energy that powered the hydrogen bomb came from which of the following?
   A splitting atoms apart
   B the collision of atoms
   C fusing atoms together
   D the creation of hydrogen atoms

9. What is massive retaliation?
   A the pledge to use overwhelming force, including nuclear weapons, to settle a serious conflict
   B the diplomatic art of going to the brink of war without actually getting into war
   C the use of firm economic control to prevent the spread of communism
   D the practice of stockpiling weapons in order to gain a military advantage over another nation

Postwar America

Test Preparation

10. What was the *Nautilus*?
    A an intercontinental ballistic missile
    B a long-range bomber aircraft
    C a nuclear-powered submarine
    D a hydrogen bomb

11. Why did the launch of *Sputnik* worry many Americans?
    A They feared it could drop bombs on them from space.
    B They feared it was spying on them.
    C They thought it meant the Soviet Union had surpassed the United States in technical skills.
    D They were afraid it would create nuclear fallout.

12. Which of the following had a major impact on politics for the first time in the 1950s?
    A radio
    B television
    C movies
    D computers

13. Which of the following first became available for commercial use in 1951?
    A computers
    B polio vaccines
    C televisions
    D bomb shelters

14. What was Levittown?
    A a part of New York City containing many apartment buildings
    B the location of the country's ICBMs
    C the town where the nuclear bomb was developed
    D a large suburban development of single-family homes

15. The Sunbelt included which region of the United States?
    A the Midwest
    B the Southwest
    C the Northeast
    D the Southeast

16. Why did women play a central role in the FCDA's civil defense program?
    A Congress was ignoring the possibility of a nuclear attack.
    B The military was too weak to protect the public.
    C Women were seen as the guardians of the home.
    D Women were less likely to be affected by nuclear fallout.

17. The arts of the 1950s often stressed which of the following?
    A prosperity
    B rebellion
    C fear of communism
    D diversity

18. Why did Michael Harrington criticize America in the postwar years?
    A He believed people living in poverty had been forgotten amid the economic successes.
    B He thought Americans were overly concerned with the possibility of a nuclear attack.
    C He saw a push toward "sameness" and the increasing loss of individuality among the growing class of business workers.
    D He thought African Americans were unfairly discriminated against.

19. **Descriptive Writing** Write a short essay describing how the 1950s were a time of both fear and optimism.

Test Preparation

The New Frontier and the Great Society — Test Preparation

1. What was the greatest difference between John F. Kennedy and Richard Nixon as presidential candidates?
   A their desire for the office
   B their stands on the Cold War
   C their personal styles
   D their ages

2. How did President Kennedy's cabinet differ from President Eisenhower's?
   A It was composed of former military officers.
   B Its members were younger.
   C It met more frequently.
   D Its members had more experience.

3. Which of the following was a result of the Bay of Pigs invasion?
   A Relations between Cuba and the United States improved.
   B Cuba's Communist regime ended.
   C The Soviet Union threatened to use military force against the United States.
   D Cuba was driven closer to the Soviet Union.

4. Why did many voters in the 1964 presidential election believe Barry Goldwater was a dangerous extremist?
   A He wanted to expand government programs to help the poor.
   B He suggested using nuclear weapons to end the war in Vietnam.
   C He strongly supported civil rights for African Americans.
   D He proposed negotiating with the Soviet Union.

5. Why was Berlin a problem for the Soviet Union?
   A It was an island of freedom surrounded by East Germany.
   B Residents of West Berlin kept sneaking into East Berlin.
   C U.S. troops were stationed in West Berlin.
   D East Germany was using force to gain control of West Berlin.

6. How did President Kennedy react to the building of the Berlin Wall?
   A He was relieved that Khrushchev would not try to seize West Berlin.
   B He thought America needed to show its strength by building up its troops.
   C He feared the possibility of nuclear war.
   D He was concerned about the East Germans who would no longer be able to escape communism.

7. Why was the Cuban missile crisis significant?
   A It caused the United Nations to outlaw nuclear weapons.
   B It pushed Soviet and U.S. leaders to become more aggressive.
   C It was the closest any nations had come to nuclear war.
   D It was a clear defeat for the United States.

8. Which of the following was one of Lyndon B. Johnson's greatest strengths?
   A his good looks
   B his charm
   C his submissive manner
   D his political experience

The New Frontier and the Great Society   Test Preparation

9. Read the quote below and answer the question that follows.

> This nation should commit itself to achieving the goal, before this decade is out, of landing a man on the moon and returning him safely to the earth. No single space project . . . will be more impressive to mankind, or more important for the long-range exploration of space . . . But in a very real sense, it will not be one man going to the moon . . . it will be an entire nation.

President Kennedy made this proposal after which event?

A The Soviet Union developed a missile that could be sent through space.

B The Soviet Union launched the first human into space.

C The Soviet Union announced its plan to develop the first space shuttle.

D A Soviet astronaut became the first person to orbit the Earth.

10. The Johnson Doctrine involved which of the following?

A intervening in revolutions in Latin America that were aimed at establishing Communist dictatorships

B strengthening conventional American forces so the nation would have other options than nuclear weapons in times of crisis

C adopting social programs to combat poverty in America

D providing economic aid to any nation that was vulnerable to a Communist takeover

11. The Warren Commission was established to investigate which of the following?

A the Cuban missile crisis

B the assassination of President Kennedy

C the Soviet space program

D the War on Poverty

12. Under the leadership of Chief Justice Earl Warren, the Supreme Court accomplished which of the following?

A extended individual rights and freedoms

B established equal rights for women

C limited the powers of Congress

D ended racial discrimination

13. Which program provided free health care to poor people?

A the Alliance for Progress

B the Economic Opportunity Act

C Medicaid

D Medicare

14. When the nation's major steel producers announced a big price increase, how did Kennedy react?

A by having Vice President Johnson put political pressure on the steel-company executives

B by issuing an executive order prohibiting price increases

C by using the media to launch a vigorous campaign against the increases

D by getting Congress to pass stricter regulations on the steel industry

15. **Persuasive Writing** Write a letter to the editor arguing either for or against the Great Society. Be sure to include examples from specific programs.

The Civil Rights Movement

Test Preparation

DIRECTIONS Read each question and circle the letter of the best response.

1. What events occurred in Watts and Detroit in the 1960s?
   A peaceful protests
   B violent riots
   C protest marches
   D civil rights rallies

2. How did the Supreme Court rule in *Brown* v. *Board of Education of Topeka, Kansas*?
   A All nine justices ruled for segregation.
   B Five justices ruled for segregation.
   C Five justices ruled against segregation.
   D All nine justices ruled against segregation.

3. Who were the Little Rock Nine?
   A African American students who tried to enroll in a white school
   B white teachers who tried to teach at an African American school
   C African American teachers who tried to teach at a white school
   D white students who tried to enroll in an African American school

4. The Civil Rights Act of 1964 did which of the following?
   A provided federal supervision over voter registration
   B banned discrimination in employment and in public accommodations
   C established a federal policy of affirmative action
   D started a jobs program in inner cities

5. The strategy of nonviolent resistance was based on the tactics used by which leader?
   A Lyndon B. Johnson
   B Mohandas Gandhi
   C Martin Luther King Jr.
   D John F. Kennedy

6. What peaceful protest tactic was used in 50 southern cities in 1960?
   A marches
   B freedom rides
   C bus boycotts
   D sit-ins

7. The Freedom Rides ended after which of the following events?
   A The federal Interstate Commerce Commission issued tough new rules forcing integration.
   B The Supreme Court declared segregation unconstitutional.
   C Martin Luther King Jr. declared the protest a success because it brought attention to the problem.
   D A violent mob attacked and killed many of the Freedom Riders.

8. Why was the Montgomery bus boycott significant?
   A Its failure led to the creation of the SCLC, which took over the boycott.
   B Its success inspired African American communities across the South.
   C Its failure encouraged Martin Luther King Jr. to shift his focus to nonviolent tactics.
   D Its success strengthened the resolve of those who opposed integration.

The Civil Rights Movement

Test Preparation

9. Read the quote from Fannie Lou Hamer. Then use this primary source and your knowledge of history to answer the following question.

> All this on account of us wanting to register, to become first-class citizens, and if the Freedom Democratic Party is not seated now, I question America. Is this America, the land of the free and the home of the brave where we have to sleep with our telephones off the hooks because our lives be threatened daily because we want to live as decent human beings in America?

What was one result of Hamer's speech at the Democratic National Convention?
A The Mississippi Freedom Democratic Party was seated at the convention.
B President Johnson promoted voting rights for African Americans.
C The split that was developing in the civil rights movement widened.
D The SCLC began to use more violent tactics.

10. What was the largest civil rights demonstration ever held in the United States?
A the March on Washington
B the Freedom Rides
C the Albany Movement
D the Birmingham campaign

11. What issue did the Twenty-fourth Amendment address?
A discrimination in employment
B voting rights
C economic inequalities
D segregation

12. What was the purpose of the Kerner Commission?
A to investigate the assassination of Martin Luther King Jr.
B to study the causes of urban rioting
C to determine the psychological effects of segregation
D to evaluate the effectiveness of civil rights legislation

13. How did Stokely Carmichael explain Black Power?
A as a call to violent action
B as an emphasis on conservatism
C as a focus on self-reliance
D as a call to racial harmony

14. Which Black Muslim minister offered a message of hope, defiance, and black pride?
A Malcolm X
B Ralph Albernathy
C Stokely Carmichael
D Martin Luther King Jr.

15. What role did TV networks play in civil rights protests?
A They demonized the protesters and their causes.
B They refused to broadcast images of the protests.
C They broadcast images of violence toward African Americans.
D They demonstrated a strong bias in favor of the protesters.

16. **Expository Writing** Write a short essay explaining what methods the civil rights movement used to protest the treatment of African Americans.

The Vietnam War   Test Preparation

DIRECTIONS Read each question and circle the letter of the best response.

1. After World War II, which nation claimed Vietnam as a colony?
   A the United States
   B the Soviet Union
   C France
   D Great Britain

2. To what did Ho Chi Minh compare Vietnam's struggle for independence?
   A the American Revolution
   B the Russian Revolution
   C World War I
   D the Cold War

3. Which event caused public opinion in America to turn against the South Vietnamese leader, Ngo Dinh Diem?
   A Diem broke up the estates of large colonial landowners and gave them to peasants.
   B Several Buddhist monks set themselves on fire to protest Diem's policies.
   C Diem's security forces tortured and imprisoned political advisers from the United States.
   D Diem publicly expressed his sympathy for the Communist cause.

4. The Tonkin Gulf Resolution did which of the following?
   A declared war on Vietnamese Communists
   B gave the president the authority to expand the war in Vietnam
   C reaffirmed Congress's constitutional right to declare war
   D declared U.S. control over the Gulf of Tonkin

5. Why did the U.S. military spray defoliants on the Vietnamese jungle?
   A to destroy enemy crops
   B to inflate the body count
   C to expose enemy supply routes and hiding places
   D to pacify opposition in the countryside

6. What was the name for the military forces of the Vietnamese Communists?
   A the Vietcong
   B the Green Berets
   C the Vietminh
   D the Khmer Rouge

7. Which of the following resulted from the American bombing campaign?
   A The flow of troops and supplies from North Vietnam to the south decreased.
   B Many South Vietnamese joined the Vietcong.
   C China and the Soviet Union cut off support to the Communist forces.
   D President Johnson scaled down the U.S. ground forces in Vietnam.

8. The U.S. military struggled with which of the following problems?
   A fighting superior troops and weapons
   B surviving the bitterly cold weather
   C acquiring enough supplies
   D identifying the enemy

9. Who served as secretary of defense for both Presidents Kennedy and Johnson?
   A Robert S. McNamara
   B Henry Kissinger
   C William Westmoreland
   D J. William Fulbright

10. How did the U.S. government attempt to reform the makeup of the military in 1969?
    A by instituting a lottery system for the draft
    B by providing deferments to men enrolled in college
    C by allowing deferments for health reasons
    D by capturing eligible young men who had escaped to Canada

11. Why was the Vietnam War called the first "living room war"?
    A because every American home was affected by the war
    B because the war was often debated in living rooms
    C because television coverage brought the war into Americans' living rooms
    D because the war revealed a "generation gap" between young Americans and their parents

12. Which of the following characterized hawks?
    A They opposed the war.
    B They supported the war's goals.
    C They supported the government's handling of the war.
    D They believed the United States was fighting against the wishes of a majority of Vietnamese.

13. Who won the 1968 presidential election?
    A John F. Kennedy
    B Richard Nixon
    C Hubert Humphrey
    D Lyndon B. Johnson

14. Why did protesters gather outside the Democratic National Convention in 1968?
    A to call for "peace with honor"
    B to demand that Johnson seek reelection
    C to express outrage at the Pentagon Papers
    D to demand an immediate end to the war

15. Why did the Tet Offensive surprise many Americans?
    A They thought the United States was winning the war.
    B They thought the Communist troops would attack urban, not rural, areas.
    C They had not expected China to enter the war.
    D They thought the Vietnamese New Year would be a time of calm.

16. What was one result of the My Lai massacre?
    A Most antiwar protesters no longer supported extremist groups or terrorist measures.
    B The divisions between war supporters and opponents intensified.
    C President Nixon began to implement the policy of Vietnamization.
    D Congress passed the War Powers Act.

17. **Narrative Writing** Write a short story about the return of an American soldier from Vietnam. Include specific problems that the main character faces.

A Time of Social Change

Test Preparation

DIRECTIONS Read each question and circle the letter of the best response.

1. What conclusion did Betty Friedan reach in her book, *The Feminine Mystique*?
   A Many women felt trapped by domestic life.
   B Women tended to receive lower wages than men did.
   C Many women felt unable to balance work and family.
   D Discrimination against women was widespread.

2. What is feminism?
   A the belief that women are superior to men
   B the conviction that women and men should be socially, politically, and economically equal
   C the desire for the fair distribution of advantages and disadvantages in society
   D the idea that women should receive special protections under the law

3. What was the result of the attempt to pass the Equal Rights Amendment?
   A It passed by a large margin.
   B It passed by a narrow margin.
   C It failed by a narrow margin.
   D It failed by a large margin.

4. Why did the pace of the feminist movement begin to slow in the late 1970s?
   A Discrimination was no longer an issue for most women.
   B Society began to reemphasize the role of women as homemakers.
   C Many working-class and nonwhite women felt that the movement did little to address their problems.
   D Many women felt that the movement had become too radical.

5. What was the significance of *Roe* v. *Wade*?
   A It protected abortion rights for women.
   B It prohibited gender discrimination in the workplace.
   C It allowed women to be drafted into the military.
   D It brought national attention to violence against women.

6. President Dwight D. Eisenhower's policy of termination involved which of the following?
   A extending antipoverty programs to Native Americans
   B cutting the ties between Native Americans and the government
   C moving Native Americans onto reservations
   D launching a media campaign to end stereotypes of Native Americans

7. Read the excerpt from the Declaration of Indian Purpose and answer the question that follows.

> Since our Indian culture is threatened by presumption of being absorbed by the American society, we believe we have the responsibility of preserving our precious heritage . . . What we ask of America is not charity . . . We ask only that the nature of our situation be recognized and made the basis of policy and action.

This declaration marked the beginning of which movement?
   A the National Indian Education movement
   B the American Indian movement
   C the Red Power movement
   D the Indian Self-Determination movement

A Time of Social Change

8. César Chávez accomplished which of the following?
   A achieved a living wage for all migrant workers
   B gained bilingual education for the children of migrant workers
   C co-founded the National Farm Workers Association
   D regained Mexican American lands from the federal government

9. How did La Raza Unida differ from the Crusade for Justice?
   A It was a political party.
   B Its members were mostly college students.
   C It supported bilingual education.
   D It used violent tactics to achieve its goals.

10. Why did the Brown Berets gain much media attention?
    A because of their success with school walkouts
    B because of their cooperation with other civil rights groups
    C because of their discrimination against women
    D because of their action-oriented protests

11. How did Cuban Americans differ from most other Latinos?
    A They believed communism was the best way to achieve social justice.
    B They left their homeland for political, not economic, reasons.
    C They were committed to political activism and ethnic pride.
    D They supported art education programs as a means of encouraging cultural development.

12. The boricua movement focused on social justice for which of the following groups?
    A migrant workers
    B Chicanos
    C Puerto Ricans
    D Cuban Americans

13. What was one complaint of the counterculture?
    A that there were not enough professional jobs available
    B that migrant workers were not receiving adequate wages
    C that the government was not doing enough to fight the spread of communism
    D that American values were hollow and its priorities were misplaced

14. The counterculture led to which of the following problems?
    A increased racial tensions
    B drug addictions and overdoses
    C obsession with war
    D close-mindedness about lifestyles and social behavior

15. What was the height of the hippie movement?
    A the Summer of Love
    B the creation of San Francisco's Haight-Ashbury District
    C the Woodstock Music and Art Fair
    D the Free Speech Movement

16. **Descriptive Writing** Write a brief essay describing how the women's, Native American, Latino, and youth social movements came to exist in the 1950s, 1960s, and 1970s.

A Search for Order | # Test Preparation

DIRECTIONS Read each question and circle the letter of the best response.

1. Conservatives favor which of the following?
   A the clear separation of church and state
   B strong opposition to communism and strict regulation of the economy
   C traditional values and less active government
   D extensive social programs

2. How did President Richard Nixon respond to growing concerns about pollution?
   A by passing legislation to regulate water pollution
   B by launching a nationwide recycling program
   C by creating the Environmental Protection Agency
   D by encouraging alternative fuel use

3. President Nixon's "southern strategy" included which of the following?
   A slowing down the enforcement of integration
   B creating more public works programs in the South
   C pushing for expanded civil rights for African Americans
   D moving factories and military bases to the South

4. How did the members of OPEC protest American support for Israel?
   A by declaring war on the United States
   B by stopping oil shipments to the United States
   C by raising the price of oil shipments to the United States
   D by officially requesting that the United States withdraw its support

5. According to the notion of realpolitik, foreign policy should be based on which of the following?
   A the protection of human rights
   B practical concerns and national interest
   C environmental concerns
   D economic goals

6. Why did President Nixon want to improve relations with China?
   A He hoped it would end communism in China.
   B He thought it would increase international trade.
   C He hoped it would end the nuclear arms race.
   D He thought it would pressure the Soviet Union into a more cooperative relationship with the United States.

7. What term refers to the ease of tension between Cold War enemies?
   A détente
   B disarmament
   C shuttle diplomacy
   D containment

8. What historic event lifted American spirits in 1969?
   A the end of segregation
   B the moon landing
   C the end of the Vietnam War
   D the Camp David Accords

9. What economic problem persisted during Nixon's second term as president?
   A tariffs
   B inflation
   C unemployment
   D debt

A Search for Order

10. The Watergate scandal began with which of the following?
    A President Nixon's refusal to hand over the White House tapes
    B the Senate committee's investigation of Nixon's campaign activities
    C charges that Vice President Spiro T. Agnew had taken payments in return for political favors
    D the burglary of the offices of the Democratic National Committee

11. Who is credited with uncovering the Watergate scandal?
    A Gerald R. Ford
    B the Federal Bureau of Investigation
    C a special prosecutor
    D two young reporters from the *Washington Post*

12. The Saturday night massacre included which of the following?
    A The special prosecutor and the attorney general quit.
    B The special prosecutor and the attorney general were fired.
    C The attorney general quit and the special prosecutor was fired.
    D The special prosecutor quit and the attorney general was fired.

13. How did President Carter try to solve the energy crisis?
    A by asking the public to conserve energy
    B by tightening government regulation of the American oil industry
    C by funding a national public transportation system
    D by ending U.S. support for Israel

14. What was one result of President Ford's pardon of Nixon?
    A Many Americans were outraged.
    B The Watergate scandal ended once and for all.
    C President Ford was required to testify before Congress.
    D Nixon could be tried in court, but not by Congress.

15. What nation did the Soviet Union invade in 1979?
    A Iran
    B Afghanistan
    C Panama
    D Israel

16. Which of the following was a top priority in President Jimmy Carter's foreign policy?
    A the end of communism
    B international trade
    C human rights
    D environmental policy

17. What occurred at Three Mile Island?
    A significant human rights abuses
    B the signing of an arms limitation agreement
    C an environmental disaster
    D the establishment of relations between Egypt and Israel

18. How did President Carter attempt to end the Iranian hostage crisis?
    A by offering to sell arms to Iran
    B by asking the UN for assistance
    C by boycotting Iranian goods
    D by approving a military mission

19. **Expository Writing** Write a brief essay explaining how Americans faced economic and political turmoil during the 1970s. Include specific examples.

A Conservative Era

Test Preparation

DIRECTIONS Read each question and circle the letter of the best response.

1. Which of the following was one of Ronald Reagan's political strengths?
   A his stage presence
   B his commitment to civil rights
   C his serious nature
   D his liberal policies

2. The New Right supported which of the following?
   A nuclear disarmament and a smaller government
   B deregulation and school prayer
   C the Equal Rights Amendment and lower taxes
   D affirmative action and the teaching of a Bible-based account of human creation

3. The name "Moral Majority" came from which of the following beliefs?
   A that the majority of government decisions should be based on morality
   B that a majority of Americans were immoral and needed guidance
   C that a majority of Americans would join the organization
   D that a majority of Americans agreed with conservative moral values

4. What is the name for the amount by which government spending exceeds government income?
   A Reaganomics
   B budget deficit
   C supply-side economics
   D recession

5. Analyze the graph below and answer the following question.

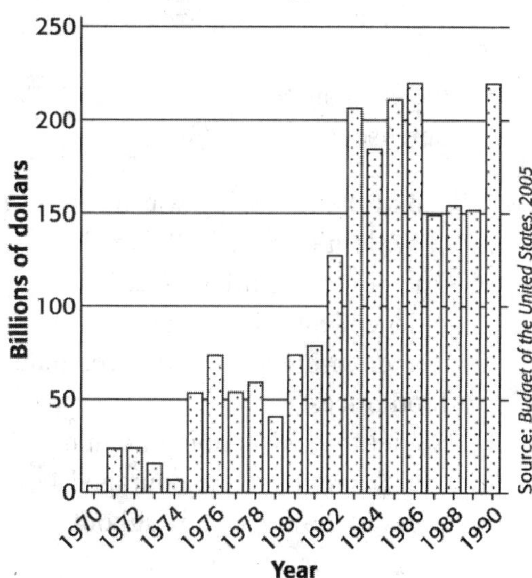

The graph illustrates the result of which of the following during the 1980s?
   A economic growth
   B low taxes and increased government spending
   C a decrease in unemployment
   D decreased interest rates

6. Why did a large number of Democrats shift their allegiance to Reagan in the elections of 1980 and 1984?
   A They found him much more trustworthy than his opponent.
   B They thought his economic policies would ensure widespread prosperity.
   C They were frustrated with the Democratic Party's stands on social and racial issues and on national security.
   D They wanted a return to the policies of Lyndon B. Johnson's Great Society.

A Conservative Era

Test Preparation

7. President Reagan obtained massive spending increases in which of the following areas?
   A education
   B energy
   C the environment
   D defense

8. Which of the following was a result of Lech Walesa's strike in Poland?
   A The government legalized independent trade unions.
   B The government began to regulate food prices.
   C Soviet troops occupied Poland.
   D The Soviet Union encouraged economic reforms throughout Eastern Europe.

9. During the 1980s, America attempted to prevent the spread of communism to which of the following nations?
   A China and South Africa
   B El Salvador and Nicaragua
   C Lebanon and Grenada
   D Iran and Afghanistan

10. Why did Mikhail Gorbachev want to strike a deal with the United States?
    A He thought it would increase his political power in the Soviet Union.
    B He wanted to increase the Soviet Union's international prestige.
    C He believed it was the only way to salvage the Soviet economy.
    D He wanted America to help reform the corrupt Soviet government.

11. In which country did the Tiananmen Square massacre occur?
    A China
    B Panama
    C Iraq
    D the Soviet Union

12. How did President Reagan put pressure on the South African government to end apartheid?
    A by implementing a policy of "constructive engagement"
    B by imposing trade limits and other sanctions
    C by threatening to use military force
    D by calling on the United Nations to supervise democratic elections

13. Which scandal exposed illegal activities within Reagan's administration?
    A the Watergate affair
    B the Iran-Contra affair
    C the Iranian hostage crisis
    D the Whitewater affair

14. What is *glasnost*?
    A lifting media censorship and allowing public criticism of the government
    B restructuring the corrupt government bureaucracy
    C building up military strength
    D adopting widespread economic reforms

15. How did Gorbachev change Soviet policy in Eastern Europe?
    A by investing heavily in the development of new industries
    B by calling for elections
    C by increasing the activity of the secret police to suppress dissent
    D by ordering a large troop pullback

16. **Persuasive Writing** Write a persuasive essay arguing either for or against Reagan's economic policy. Be sure to include specific details and facts.

Test Preparation

Into the Twenty-First Century

Test Preparation

---

1. Which of the following was a high priority for President Bill Clinton?
   A a stronger military
   B health-care reform
   C lower taxes
   D an end to affirmative action

2. The Contract with America included plans for which of the following?
   A cutting taxes and fighting crime
   B increasing funding for education
   C reforming health-care
   D cutting the military budget

3. The Dayton Accords aimed at ending fighting in which country?
   A Haiti
   B Bosnia and Herzegovina
   C Somalia
   D Israel

4. President Clinton's welfare-reform plan included which of the following?
   A an increase in the time people could receive benefits
   B an extension of benefits to single mothers
   C a requirement that most recipients find work within two years of getting benefits
   D a limit on the number of people who could qualify for the program

5. Which agreement made the United States, Canada, and Mexico one large free trade zone?
   A the World Trade Agreement
   B the North American Free Trade Agrewent
   C the North Atlantic Treaty Agreement
   D the General Agreement on Tariffs and Trade

6. Study the graph below and answer the following question.

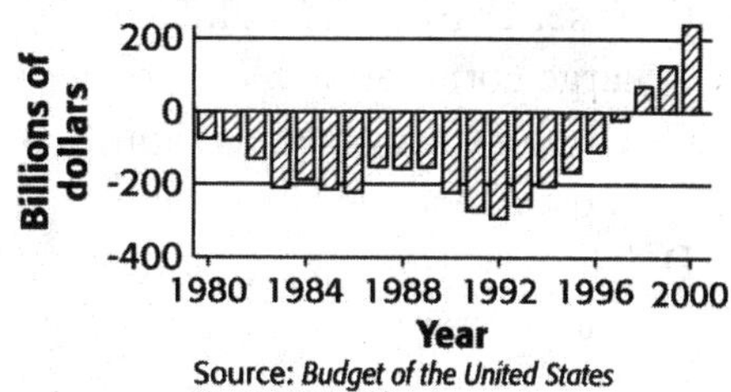

What does this graph demonstrate about the federal budget under President Clinton?
   A Clinton entered office with a deficit and created a surplus.
   B Clinton entered office with a surplus and created a deficit.
   C Clinton balanced the budget every year.
   D Clinton's management of the budget was inconsistent.

7. In the presidential election of 2000, who ran as the leader of the Green Party?
   A Dick Cheney
   B Ralph Nader
   C H. Ross Perot
   D Joe Lieberman

8. In *Bush* v. *Gore*, why did the U.S. Supreme Court rule that the Florida Supreme Court's recount order was unconstitutional?
   A because it violated the right to privacy
   B because the recount would only occur in heavily Democratic areas
   C because it failed to provide clear standards by which the ballots were to be counted
   D because none of the disputed ballots were valid

                                          Test Preparation

9. What is one reason the stock market dropped in the early 2000s?
   A Successful dot-coms took over many large businesses.
   B A series of scandals hit several large corporations.
   C High taxes limited the ability of most Americans to invest.
   D The government began to regulate the stock market more closely.

10. Why did some Americans criticize the White House Office of Faith-Based Initiatives?
   A The office only provided federal funding to Christian organizations.
   B They believed that the states should be in charge of funding community-service organizations.
   C They worried that the program might cross the constitutional line separating church and state.
   D They wanted the funds used by the office to go toward improvements in education.

11. What was a top priority for George W. Bush's second term as president?
   A reform of Social Security
   B protection of the environment
   C deficit reduction
   D reform of the health-care system

12. How did the U.S. government attempt to combat terrorism at home?
   A by closing some forms of public transportation
   B by passing gun control and weapons regulations
   C by strengthening the powers of law-enforcement
   D by stationing the military around the country

13. Read the quote from President Bush and answer the question that follows.

> We're a peaceful nation. Yet, as we have learned, so suddenly and so tragically, there can be no peace in a world of sudden terror. In the face of today's new threat, the only way to pursue peace is to pursue those who threaten it.

In this speech, President Bush is announcing a military attack against which nation?
   A Afghanistan
   B Iraq
   C Iran
   D Israel

14. Why does health care present some of the greatest challenges for the future?
   A Medical researchers have been unsuccessful at combating deadly diseases.
   B The cost of medical care and insurance is rising.
   C The government refuses health-care coverage to most Americans.
   D Health care frequently conflicts with environmental concerns.

15. Which of the following demonstrated the vulnerability of the American people and economy to disaster?
   A HIV/AIDS
   B genetic engineering
   C the energy crisis
   D Hurricane Katrina

16. **Expository Writing** Write a short essay explaining how the U.S. population is expected to change in coming decades.